When Michigan Was Young

DEDICATED

to the Ottawas and Ojibways of L'Arbre Croche and their loyal sons who have given their lives in the service of their country in all conflicts in which it has been engaged since their enfranchisement as citizens of Michigan.

E.R.F.

When Michigan Was Young

The Story of Its Beginnings, Early Legends, and Folklore

By
Ethel Rowan Fasquelle

Avery Color Studios
AuTrain, Michigan 49806

WHEN MICHIGAN WAS YOUNG
by Ethel Rowan Fasquelle
Copyright 1981, by Avery Color Studios
AuTrain, Michigan 49806
Library of Congress #81-66875
ISBN 0-932212-22-0

First Edition - 1981
Reprinted - 1983, 1986, 1987

All rights in this book are reserved. No part may be reproduced in any manner without permission in writing from the publisher, except brief quotations for review purposes.

When Michigan Was Young was first published in 1950 by Wm. B. Eerdman Publishing Company, Grand Rapids, Michigan. Their permission has been granted for this reprint.

PREFACE

The story of Michigan is written here because thousands of people have been asking for it these many years. Since the casual reader has little time for prodigious historical tones, it is to meet the desire for a condensed and accurate knowledge of this great Ottawa Land and Inner Empire that this contribution to Michigan's history has been written.

The discovery in 1634 of this country from which so many of our states were carved followed closely on the heels of the landing of the Puritan Fathers on Plymouth Rock. Because of its isolation, civilization in the Inner Empire came slowly. It was not until after the Dutch had broken the Iroquois wall between the east and west by their purchase of vast tracts of land from the Six Nations in western New York, that civilization began to rise in the Great Lakes region. With the opening of the Erie Canal a flood of migration from the east set in toward the new states of the ancient Inner Empire. This trek toward the west was so great that it was found when genealogists set to work building the many patriotic organizations which now exist in Michigan, that more descendants of colonial blood were to be found in Michigan than in most of the seaboard States. So it may easily be seen that what goes on, and has gone on in Michigan in the years past is of vital interest to the entire nation.

The name Ottawa Land was often applied to Michigan because the aboriginal Ottawa nation, descendants of the Algonuins, claimed hundreds of thousands of acres of land as their own private hunting preserve in this limitless Inner Empire; ranging from the Straits of Michilimackinac west to the Dakotas and to the Ohio River on the south. The Ojibways, or Chippewas, also descendants of the Algonquins, with the fighting Iroquois ever at their back, joined the Ottawas several hundred years ago. Once numbering many hundreds of thousand, the two nations have lived together for many generations as one nation.

We have tried to portray the life and habits of the aboriginal peoples and to tell their stories and legends, and their history in so far as the progress of civilization was affected by their contact with the white race.

Michigan's Indians are a valued part of the state's life today, with both men and women given their voting franchise. Michigan's evolution from a vast aboriginal Inner Empire from which most of the Middle Western States were separated, to its present position of prestige among the States of the nation in a little over three hundred years since its discovery by Jean Nicolet in 1634, forms one of the most important of the epics in our national history.

E.R.F.

Petoskey, Michigan
July 10, 1950

CONTENTS

PART I

Michigan's Historic Past

From the French Explorer's Claim of New France in North America, 1534, to the Realization of Michigan's Statehood, 1837.

Chapter One 13
    New France in North America is Founded by Jacques Cartier, 1534.

Chapter Two 17
    Jean Nicolet Discovers the Straits of Michilimackinac, 1634.

Chapter Three 26
    The Beaver Rules an Empire

Chapter Four 31
    The English Capture the Inner Empire.

Chapter Five 38
    Michilimackinac Territory Becomes Michigan Territory.

Chapter Six 44
    The State of Michigan Enters the Union, 1837.

PART II

Ancient Guardians of the Straits of Michilimackinac

From the First Fort in Michilimackinac Soon After Nicolet's Discovery of the Straits in 1634 to the Present Date.

Chapter Seven 51
    Nicolet Discovers the Straits of Michilimackinac

Chapter Eight 56
    The First Guardian of the Straits

Chapter Nine 62
    Fort Michilimackinac

Chapter Ten 69
    The British Appear in Michilimackinac

Chapter Eleven 76
    American Posession of Fort Mackinac

Chapter Twelve 83
    The Last Guardian of the Straits of Michilimackinac

PART III

Families and Customs — Stories and Legend

How the Ancient Ottawas and Ojibways lived and Their Names, Customs and Legends. Stories of the First White Settlers of Early Michigan, and Indian Legends, Ending with the Modern True Story of Joe Francis' Heroism.

Chapter Thirteen The First Families of Michilimackinac.	88
Chapter Fourteen What's In a Name?	100
Chapter Fifteen The Passing of the Neuter Nation.	106
Chapter Sixteen Corn, The Indian's Staff of Life.	109
Chapter Seventeen The Legend of Ne-Naw-Bo-Zhoo.	118
Chapter Eighteen Pokagon's Village	123
Chapter Nineteen The A.B.C.'s of the Rev. Peter Dougherty.	129
Chapter Twenty Muh-quh Se-bing, or The Bear Walk.	138
Chapter Twenty-one Joe Francis, Hero.	146

PART I

MICHIGAN'S HISTORIC PAST

Chapter One

New France in North America is founded by Jacques Cartier, 1534

Since the beginning of time Mother Earth has swayed the destinies of her children with the products of her soil or her forests and waters. What at first appeared to be trifles have sent men wandering over the face of the earth ever searching for one product or another. During the Middle Ages spices for the preservation of meats and other foods were a necessity for the European nations. With wars constantly being waged at home and abroad, food supplies and their protection were of the utmost importance. But spices in quantity came only from the Oriental countries, and at the opening of the seventeenth century Portugal, at that time a mighty seafaring power, controlled the route to China and India.

It was in search of a western passage that Christopher Columbus, Sir Walter Raleigh, the Cabots, and all the other great navigators sailed to the western shores of the Atlantic Ocean. In the year 1533 Jacques Cartier, Vice

When Michigan Was Young

Admiral of France, sailed out of the port of St. Malo in France, ostensibly on a fishing trip, with three ships in his fleet. But while the fish were expected to defray the expenses of the voyage, the real quest was the western passage from the Atlantic to the China Sea.

Cartier anchored in the Bay of Gaspe off the coast of Newfoundland in North America, the first explorer to report a contact so far north in which natives were encountered. He promptly called the land New France in North America. To prove his adventure the French admiral carried several of the natives home with him. However, the poor natives soon died in their new environment and Cartier did not receive the cordial welcome when he returned to New France the following year. But he did learn of a great water flowing away toward the west from the ocean farther down the coast. And he sailed directly toward it discovering the mouth of the St. Lawrence river in the year 1534.

We have little concern with the events of the next seventy years when fishing seems to have absorbed the French adventurers who followed after Cartier and who evidently found the Indian inhabitants of the land too hostile and the difficulties of navigation down the St. Lawrence too hazardous to encounter. But we do have concern with the establishment of the Fort of Quebec, or Kebec, by Samuel de Champlain, in 1608, eight hundred miles from the mouth of the St. Lawrence toward the west. That opened up the western passage, not to the Orient, but to the Great Lakes and lands beyond of which no man had ever dreamed before. This was a much more important event to our minds than the discovery of a quick passage to the lands of spices.

And now like the turning of a weather vane, though with that old desire for the lands of spices underlying

New France in North America Founded in 1534

other motives, a small creature of the forest directs the progress of man toward the west. The beautiful pelt of the beaver becomes the object of the voyageurs of New France; and the thousands of lakes and streams bordering on the St. Lawrence river abound in beaver. Almost in twinkling of an eye the crafty little beaver becomes the dominant factor in the new land, even for more than a hundred years passing as its currency. It is of historical note that the beaver played a greater part in opening the middle western country than any other one factor.

We must voyage back to Europe and to France to find the secret of this sudden change, yet it really was not so sudden; for furs from America had been crossing the sea to Europe for more than half a century before the insignificant little beaver set itself up as an arbiter of the fashions of France, and caused the revival of the fur trade in that country and New France that had lanquished for many years.

It is a far cry from the hat of a French King of more than three hundred years ago to the great State of Michigan of 1950. The banquet halls of France were cold drafty places, and the head of Louis XIII was no doubt cold. He may have had a touch of our modern flu when he wore his gorgeous chapeau of beaver fur into the festive hall. At any rate the king unwittingly created a fashion that set two continents agog, and changed the destiny of the western world.

We find the roots of Michigan in the archives of Louis XIII and Louis XIV of France, in their luxury loving courts and the need of their treasuries for funds to support their excesses and extravagances. It was the wiley brain of Richelieu, minister of foreign affairs for Louis XIII, that found a way to extract large sums of money from the fashionable young nobles of France who were following the king in the use of costly furs for personal adornment.

Also, as cardinal of the Catholic church Richelieu was eager to establish New France as an absolute Catholic colony. And then there was that old matter of spices. The army had to have them for the preservation of foods; and the need to discover that still elusive western passage to China and the Indies entered large in his plans.

Chapter Two

Jean Nicolet Discovers the Straits of Michilimackinac, 1634

New France had been in existence since 1534 when Jacques Cartier had landed his fishing fleet in the Bay of Gaspe off the coast of Newfoundland and had claimed the land adjacent to it as New France in North America. But there had never been a minister of foreign affairs in France strong enough and clever enough to finance the development of this faraway new land.

Richelieu was one of the most powerful men in Europe, and when he requested memberships for his Organization of One Hundred Associates among the wealthy nobles it was more or less a command, and the rush for the new world was on. Not like the rush for the gold of California in 1849, with its free-for-all rough and tumble desire of every man to get there first, but a carefully planned and royally financed adventure entered into with gay enthusiasm by the finest courtiers of France, many of whom shipped as sailors to ensure their passage to the new land.

When Michigan Was Young

Samuel de Champlain, soldier, sailor, fur trader, and explorer, was appointed governor of New France and representative of the new company which was to become the first get-rich-quick scheme in North America. Champlain had spent years in New France as commandant of the Fort of Quebec, and had great influence among the Indian hunters along the great river that divided the continent. But he had never been able to penetrate as far as the big waters that the Indians assured him lay beyond the wall of the fierce fighting Iroquois and their confederates.

There had been a young Frenchman who had lived among the Indians for ten years who knew more of their languages and dialects than any other man in New France. His remarkable aptitude for languages and his methods of square dealing in fur trading had won him the friendship of many of the nations and tribes. No man in New France was nearer to the Indians than Jean Nicolet. It was natural that Champlain should select Nicolet to head this hazardous expedition into the west in search of the long-sought passage leading to the eastern spice countries. It may be well to explain here that the reason French expeditions did not go directly east from France was that the powerful Portuguese controlled both overland and sea roadways to China and the Indies. Both the English and the French were seeking desperately a way to get to the East without encountering the Portuguese; the English by way of the Northwest Passage through Hudson's Bay, and the French by the Western Passage by way of New France. The two passages are very often confused although they were quite different.

So we find Commandant Champlain and the young Jean Nicolet making plans during the winter of 1633 and 1634 for the great adventure. Nicolet was to meet as

Jean Nicolet Discovers Straits of Michilimackinac

many western Indians as could be brought together by fleet runners at a neutral point bordering on the great waters of the west, thought by all to be the Pacific Ocean. There was to be a grand council and treaties were to be signed—a very heavy responsibility for a man still under thirty. We know this fact because we know that Jean Nicolet left France at the age of eighteen, and that he had spent ten years among the Indians trading and studying the Indian languages, and at the same time making firm friends of hundreds of them.

Elaborate plans were made for the journey which was to be by way of the inner route leading among hundreds of islands, using many portages connecting rivers and lakes, and doing most of the traveling by night to avoid the ever dreaded Iroquois and their allies. The party set out from Three Rivers, on the St. Lawrence, in the spring of 1634 in a heavily laden pirogue bound for the big waters of which the Hunter Indians had told them.

A pirogue was a boat made from the heart of a giant tree, sometimes fifty feet in length. It was much heavier than a batteau or a canoe, designed for heavy loads while at the same time carrying from ten to fifteen passengers. The cargo for this expedition consisted mostly of gifts for the counciling chiefs and their families. The pirogues were equipped with both paddles and sails, the latter made of bark that had been carefully prepared and woven together with thongs made of animal skins.

The boats required expert handling, often in and out of small passages, to avoid the dangers of the trip. On the upper side of the St. Lawrence were the Algonquins, and on the lower side the Iroquois, both deadly enemies of the milder tempered Hunter Indians, so named by the French fur traders. They were probably one of the many off-shoots of the Algonquins endeavoring to get away from their savage wranglings.

In August of 1634 the adventurers landed at the Indian village of Taenhotentaron—the point that we know now as St. Ignace—on the Straits of Mackinac, which was at that time an unnamed body of water but quickly discernible as not being a great ocean. This point was at that time a neutral meeting place for all the tribes of the big lakes and northern rivers to come to discuss their difficulties in arbitration, a sort of United Nations Council headquarters in the heart of a hostile land.

Several localities have laid claim to the exact spot where was held this Grand Council, which was to determine the destiny of the inland seas. Jean Nicolet had lived close to the Indians and must have known that this point was the only safe place for his small party of seven hunters to meet with thousands of savages.

The writer has been unable to find an affirmation of this meeting's exact place in a careful search of the French Relations of that period. The only comment found is a casual one sent back to France by a Jesuit priest, as follows: "And Nicolet went down into the country of the Baye des Puants, and there was a council held with the Indians." This single sentence, written with the dividing comma, is the entire authority that can be presented for the claim that the council was held in the land of the Puant nation, known to be a canibalistic people. They were later to be known as the Winnebagoes, or Tobacco Indians.

Nicolet's own notes, if he made any, must have been lost, for only the projected plans for the trip and his directions to stop at this neutral point have survived. But it is recorded that there was a meeting between Jean Nicolet and his seven companions and at least five thousand Indians. Nicolet, messenger of the king of France,

Jean Nicolet Discovers Straits of Michilimackinac

appeared before this great host in the robes of a Chinese mandarin, supposedly to arouse in the minds of the Indians recollections of the Eastern lands from which it was believed they came.

In Nicolet's hands were held, high above his head, two great pistols, and as he approached the gathering he fired both of the pistols into the air. It was a dramatic thing to do, but very strange and dangerous, for it nearly cost the lives of the entire group of white men. Many of the Indians had never heard of this deadly "fire and thunder," and there was a near-panic. But friendly Indians who had traded their furs to Nicolet many times at the Three Rivers post promptly interceded and explained that this was the white man's way of saluting and paying them honor.

The council went on to a friendly settlement, closing with the usual pipe of peace and the signing of the first treaty ever made in the Great Lakes country, henceforth to be called the Province of Michilimackinac. The treaty gave the King of France jurisdiction over all of the vast hunting grounds claimed by these people, the largest and leading nation presently to be known as the Ottawa nation.

And thus there was born, in one of the most dramatic moments in the history of the United States, the great Inner Empire of Michilimackinac in New France, in the heart of the domain eventually to be divided into what we now call the Middle Western States of the United States.

After paying a visit to the sacred Island of the Ottawas, which we know as Mackinac Island, Nicolet continued on toward the west and south into the country of the Illinese. He must have learned on this trip that the big water of which they had been told was a river running north and south, with great hunting lands beyond, for we find no more mention of a connection between the North American Indians and the Chinese. That idea was now to be forgotten until in our own day, when speculation as to the truth of the matter is launched occasionally by students of research in ethnological origins.

The story of the Jean Nicolet expedition has been told at length because Nicolet was the first man to set foot on what was to become the soil of the State of Michigan.

Michigan should be proud to accept Jean Nicolet as its first great hero and all honor should be paid him as the man who opened the Straits of Mackinac and the great west beyond to commerce. From that day to the present time the straits have played an important part in the commerce and the progress of the west.

The death of Samuel de Champlain on Christmas Day of 1635 removed the impelling force behind the development of the western part of New France, and the project was dropped for some years. But Jean Nicolet had opened the back door of New France, and had found an entirely new land for its enrichment in what was now to be called the Province of Michilimackinac in New France. It was to consist of all lands west of the Straits of Mackinac and to the south as far as the hunting grounds of the Indians reached.

The territory was so vast that no man dreamed of its size, and was so full of fur-bearing animals that when once a garrison had been established, a flood of voyageurs and adventurers swept into the lake regions and hundreds of thousands of dollars worth of furs found their way through the trading posts and on to the mother country across the ocean. In fact, from one to five thousand hunters went up the St. Lawrence together in great convoys with their cargoes of rich pelts for market. More than a hundred thousand skins were known to have been

Jean Nicolet Discovers Straits of Michilimackinac

sent out in one year. They were beaver, bear, fox, otter, musquash, (muskrat), marten, kitt fox, minx, lynx, wolverine, fisher, racoon, wolf, elk, deer, buffalo, moose and numerous other furs. The country of the Great Lakes was being peopled, but not colonized in the true sense of that word. It started as a big commercial enterprise and deviated little from that idea for more than a century.

The dream of finding a passage to the Orient through New France was not abandoned until after Marquette and Joliet had made their great discovery of the Mississippi's headwaters in 1693. It is the belief that Jean Nicolet never thought, after his first meeting with the western Indians, that such a passage existed, at least at any possible distance that could be traversed by man in that day.

Nicolet seemed to feel that he had ended his great mission. He had made a treaty with the Indians of the west and had opened up a vast territory to commerce. He had prepared the way for the missionaries of his faith to come into that country without fear. And he must have learned to his own satisfaction that the water to the west was not an ocean, but a great river flowing north and south. And that was not what he was seeking. He was told that there were more hunting grounds beyond, why then should he go on? After a visit to the Illinese he returned to his post at Three Rivers, and it is probable that plans were under way for a return trip to the Straits another spring. But the death of Champlain in 1635 put a stop to further exploration and exploitation of the west at that time. Nicolet's death in 1642 removed another strong factor in the development of trade relations with the western Indian tribes.

Jean Nicolet lost his life while trying to swim to the assistance of an Indian friend who had been captured by the Iroquois and was about to be put to death. Of the character of this first white man to set foot on Michigan soil, Campbell, the Jesuit priest and historian, speaks in the highest terms. He describes him as having been of the old Apostolic type of Christian, a man of the finest sense of justice and admirable in every way. The Indians worshipped him, almost as a God, because they understood this. Their grief at his death was almost inconsolable, for they realized that they had lost their best friend among the white traders.

This Nicolet story has been elaborated upon because it is Michigan's foundation story, the beginning of its history. Until recent years it was scarcely known because of the very small amount of reference material, and its inaccessibility. There has been a tremendous change in contact with source material in the last several decades.

Trees "chopped" down by beavers to be "nosed" to the dam under construction in the background.

Chapter Three

The Beaver Rules an Empire

During the next half century after Nicolet's western voyage, forts, trading posts, and missions with small villages surrounding them sprang up throughout the Province of Michilimackinac bordering on the inland seas. The Straits region became a beehive of commerce, and continued its leadership for more than one hundred years. Isolated by the human wall of savages that encircled its southern and western boundaries, the struggle for independence on the Atlantic seaboard affected this Inner Empire not at all. It was a period that might well be chronicled as the rape of the forests, for wild animals were slaughtered like rats, by the thousands, for greed and gain.

At the same time the Indians were being debauched and degraded by the use of "fire water," and scandalously cheated by an almost uncontrolled system of trading. During all these years of barter and trade with the Indians, the currency of the land was the beaver skin, the most highly valued of all the pelts brought to the trading posts.

The unfairness of the trader in his dealings with the Indians is almost unbelievable, and in a measure exonorates them for their childish resentment when they realized this. If an Indian wished to purchase a rifle, he had to bring in a pile of beaver pelts that would reach from stock of the rifle, resting on the ground, to the barrel of the weapon. To insure a good deal, rifles were often made with stock six feet in length. A very splendid deal for the trader, who secured hundreds of dollars worth of furs valued at thousands of francs in France. The traders called these long rifles "Beaver Rifles."

What may be an explanation of this sort of dealing is found in one of Henry Schoolcraft's histories. He tells us that the Indian never sold anything; that buying and selling was a science utterly unknown to the aborigines. All property exchanges were in the form of gifts. Whatever the recipient had to give was all right. Shells, crude weapons, one of his wives or a child, or a pony, something that seemed to him a like value for what he had received. Intentional defrauding received severe punishment. The trader played upon this ancient custom to his own advantage.

The treasury of Louis XIII had never been a full one. But Louis XIV had come into power in 1643 a wealthy boy. When he gained full power as king this fact was to have a remarkable effect upon the Province of Michilimackinac. This Louis loved conquest and power, and wanted a widespread domain. The policies of Richelieu were to be continued and enlarged upon by Mazarin, the minister of Louis XIV.

The persecutions of the Huguenots in the later years of the reign of Louis XIV were to send thousands of sincerely

The Beaver Rules an Empire

pious people to the new land in search of homes and peace. Interest sprang up again in the fur industry in New France and stronger forces were sent to maintain the forts at the trading posts, the most outlying of these being Michilimackinac Post located at the Indian village, Taenhotentaron, now St. Ignace.

Pushed by the Sioux in Canada, the Ottawas and Ojibways were being forced down into the Straits country. In the summer of 1669 the great chief of the Ojibways, or Chippewas, Wabojeeg by name, whose granddaughter became the wife of Henry Schoolcraft, brought a thousand of his warriors and their families to Michilimackinac in search of a new home.

With them came the Jesuit priest, Pere Jacques Marquette, who at once set about to build a mission and church on what was known as the Pointe. His is a story that is too well known for this writer to add anything to its glory. It was not a well known story until less than a century ago. Very old histories barely mention Marquette so jealously was source material kept from prying eyes by the church in earlier days.

The Ottawas and Ojibways were both major branches of the Algonquin nation living in lower Canada. It is said that when these tribes first met as antagonists in the Great Lakes country, their surprise that they could understand almost every word of each other's language pleased them so much that they threw down their war clubs and at once smoked the pipe of peace, and forever after were allies in their wars against the Sioux and the Iroquois, deadly enemies of both nations.

When the English first came among the Algonquins they were told of a tribe of that nation that had gone "out-aways," as they comprehended the word. Thereupon they spoke of these people as "Od-a-ways," and the

French as usual had a name for it and called them Ottawas, a name that was accepted and has been retained to the present time. These people once roamed over the entire territory that was to become the Territory of Michilimackinac, but were at last crowded into a home on Mackinac Island, with scattered branches on other islands in the Great Lakes.

With the end of the seventeenth century the story of the Territory of Michilimackinac became a divided one, and the lower portion at the foot of the lakes took on a new stride. Antoine de la Mothe Cadillac commandant of the garrison at the Pointe, known as Iroquois Pointe, now St. Ignace, quarreled bitterly with the Jesuits over his reckless exploitations of the Indians in his ambition to increase the fur trade. Cadillac's conflict with the Jesuits began soon after his arrival there about 1695.

By the end of that decade Cadillac had secured permission from the king to set up a new fort and trading post farther south. In 1701 Cadillac moved his garrison to his new fort at Detroit, and called it Fort Ponchartrain. He invited the Indians to the north and to the west of him to settle around the new fort, and soon the fur trade began to flourish, unhampered by the scruples of the Jesuits. However lack of harmony among the Indians themselves together with Cadillac's Janis-faced dealings with the mutually hostile Ottawas and Miamies seriously alienated these tribes from the French causing them much trouble years later. Cadillac commanded at Fort Ponchartrain ten years, when he was sent to New Orleans by the French government. He remained there several years until his recall to France, where he died a few years later.

The Jesuits had worked long and hard for their slow progress in the north and appealed to the governor of

The Beaver Rules an Empire

Canada for another post at the Straits. The French, at second glance, realized that it was necessary to reestablish a post on the Straits lest they lose both Indians and precious furs in this whole upper region to the English. And in 1715 Fort Michilimackinac was built on the south shore of the Straits where Mackinac City now is located.

However, much of the population of the straits sought out the greater safety of Mackinac Island where Indians and Frenchmen and women lived an almost idyllic life. For all during these years, nearly a century, marriages between the Frenchmen and the beautiful Indian girls had been going on, until it was said that only a few hundred Ottawas could, through unmixed heredity, use the moose, the totem of the Ottawas, as their tribal animal.

French traders with Indian wives had made substantial fortunes in the fur trade, and their children were being sent to Quebec and Montreal to be educated and later many of the young girls were even sent to convent schools in France. But when they returned to the Island, and in turn married some young French voyageur, or a half-breed, they resumed the old mode of living in many ways, mixing the household gadgets of civilization with the primitive in an amazing way. But they were all most beautifully happy, and their island home became a sort of Arcadia to them.

Chapter Four

The English Capture the Inner Empire

Conditions were quite different in the region of Detroit from those in the upper country of the Straits. In the lower country of the Inner Empire all was strife, intrigue, battle and tragedy, and wars and dissentions with the Indians aggravated by the ignorance of governors who knew nothing of the characteristics of the Indians. They were usually men of arrogance whom the home offices wanted to get rid of, and so they were sent to this out-of-the-way post. The entire conduct of what was now the Territory of Michilimackinac was something rather scandalous. Both civil governors and commandants at the forts insisted upon what they considered their prestige, with the Indians never knowing whom to obey, and always being appeased with whiskey and brandy, which of course only made matters worse.

Because of their protests, the Jesuit priests, whose control of the Indians of the Straits had wielded an influence for good, were given to understand that too much

The English Capture the Inner Empire

of their interference was not needed in the southern area. St. Anne's Church in Detroit is one of the few relics of their persistence and efforts to set the standard of the church permanently in the lower frontier settlements.

And so matters went, from bad to worse, until on the 13th of September, 1759, the capture of Quebec by General Wolfe broke the power of France in the great Inner Empire that the French had held in America for more than a century. In the fifty-eight years that the French had occupied Detroit there had been eighteen commandants at the fort. When the British took it over, under Major Rogers, there were a few hundred dwellings and over a thousand people in the village and the fort.

A notable visit to Detroit about this time brought many changes to the locality. Sir William Johnson, the ablest British Indian agent in America, was sent from the east to Detroit to straighten out the tangles between officials and Indians, and the affair was made much of, and seems to be registered as the high event of the period. Captain Henry Gladwin was now put in charge of the post and things went smoothly for a time.

Intermarriages between the French and the Indians for many years had brought understanding of characteristics on both sides, but the English were arrogant toward the natives and refused them powder and the lavish gifts which characterized the more convivial French. The Indians were a mixture of Ottawas, Pottawattamies, and numerous other tribes of the west, and a difficult group of people to handle. And now with the English in power over the French, the Indians quickly learned the contemptible part they must play under the cold, arrogant treatment of British colonial hauteur. When the growing unrest and hostility of the natives came to a head, Indian leaders, with agitation from the French, began to hold war councils in a plan to throw off the English yoke. In 1763, Pontiac, an Ottawa chieftain, along with other Indian leaders chafing under British domination led their warriors in a series of massacres against the English, seizing all their western forts and villages from Wisconsin to Pennsylvania but three: Niagara, Fort Pitt and Detroit. In this uprising Pontiac undertook the siezure of Detroit, the strongest of all the western posts.

At Detroit it happened that a young French girl had a lover in the fort to whom she told the plan as she had learned it from half-breed relatives, but in a way that they did not realize. The girl betrayed the story to the young soldier and Major Gladwin was well prepared to intercept the plans of Pontiac, which he did with success, and the fort was saved. The Pontiac raid was a very long and tragic one, one of its results being the destruction of Fort Pequotenonce at the present Mackinaw City on the Straits of Mackinac.

It has been believed that this French girl was an Indian woman, mistress of Major Gladwin, but this myth has been thoroughly investigated, and Mr. Catlin, a Michigan historian, discredits it absolutely, in favor of the one discovered more recently regarding the young officer.

Pontiac's siege of Detroit lasted one hundred and fifty-three days before help arrived to rescue the fort and settlement from its Indian besiegers. Major Gladwin commanded the fort during this siege, and among those caught under its protection was Robert Navarre, who had been the most successful of all the French governors prior to the reoccupation by the English. Navarre was a direct descendant of Henry IV of France, and a man of much ability. All during the long days of this fearsome time he kept a diary recording the daily events and conditions within the fort, a most remarkable record.

The English Capture the Inner Empire

This manuscript was found many years later tucked between the rafters of the attic of his cabin, and was referred to at some length by Henry Schoolcraft, the historian, in one of his books. The first translator of this document was Professor Louis Fasquelle, founder of the Chair of Languages at the University of Michigan, at Ann Arbor, Michigan. The original manuscript is in the Burton Historical Library now owned by the city of Detroit. It is called the Pontiac Diary and is considered one of the state's most valuable documents, as it provides the source material for our knowledge of the happenings during what is regarded as Michigan's most tragic episode.

For several years after the massacre of Fort Pequotenonce there was no garrison on the Straits, but the fur trade continued, and in the late 1700's we find both the Hudson's Bay Company doing business there, and the Northwestern Fur Company creeping westward as it encroached upon the domain of the Hudson's Bay hunters. Life went on at the Island of Mackinac almost as if war were an unheard-of thing. In fact, it was becoming rather a brilliant frontier gathering in this out-of-the-way settlement. Men of real ability and women of much charm were members of the Island colony.

The English had erected a small fort at the old Mackinac location sometime in the 1760's but when Captain Patrick Sinclair arrived to take command of it he found it a most dilapidated place, having been garrisoned only intermittently. Straightway he began plans for its removal to the Island. This he accomplished in the year 1783, occupying what was then called Fort George or Fort Mackinac as we know it today.

Considering the fact that Sinclair built this fort after the Revolutionary War had been fought, and the Treaty of Paris of 1783 had been signed between the British and Americans, and numerous other treaties also, the insistence of the English to continue occupation of the country was exceedingly strange, even in those days of slow communication. It is difficult to realize that it took a year or more to effect the journey from England to the Straits.

Dr. W. B. Hinsdale of the University of Michigan at Ann Arbor traced fifteen trails, or Indian highways, coming into Michigan from all directions, and these were linked to thousands of Indian villages all over the country. Water was the only other means of travel, and in winter that was not practical. Michigan lay in a most hazardous position, and that is one of the reasons for its late admission as a state.

In the later 1700's the Americans had about exhausted their resources. There wasn't much fight left in them, but Benjamin Franklin was predicting that the Michigan situation with the English would not end without another war to settle the differences.

Still the English went on unmolested and did their hunting, fort building, and everything else that they were pleased to do, even attaching the Detroit area to the county of Kent in Canada, until it finally dawned upon the men in the Congress of the United States that this was their playground. The aggressive young settlers to the west who had pleaded with them for help so endlessly were at last heeded.

As late as 1784, Haldimand, the English governor, was building sawmills and gristmills at Detroit and along the St. Clair shores; at the same time however, he continued to offer resistance to white settlers coming into the Ohio Valley.

There had been extensive grants of wild land given by

The English Capture the Inner Empire

the United States Congress to the eastern states under organized groups of the big landowners and politicians. One of these groups was headed by Thomas Lee of Virginia, and the Lees were men of great power in the east. Massachusetts also had extensive claims, as did other states, though of less extent. These matters were contributory to the final decision of the Congress to stop the treaty bickerings and step out in the open and take what belonged to the United States.

There had been several worthless treaties with the Indians, and several signed with the English since the close of the Revolution. At last, however, in 1794, General Anthony Wayne, "Mad Anthony Wayne," finally secured the Northwest from the Indians when he decisively defeated them at the battle of Fallen Timbers, near present Toledo, Ohio. On the way a regiment of Kentucky Rangers, seasoned Indian fighters, was picked up. These men were well accustomed to the hardships of the woods and were mostly big fellows; and whenever they went they meant business.

The story of this march to the north is a thrilling one. Like burning grass they swept everything before them, ending in an ambush of the savages that gained one more name for Wayne, "The Black Snake." For with a force only a third as large as that of the Indians he completely encircled their camps and cut off help from the fort's besiegers and effected the rescue of the fort at last. There had been 2,000 Indians in the battle, while Wayne's forces numbered less than 900. This was one of the decisive battles that was to settle finally the supremacy of the Americans in the Great Lakes region. However, not until the war of 1812 with the British did the Americans fully gain absolute control of this territory.

During this period the Inner Empire was variously

known as the Province of Michilimackinac, Territory of Michilimackinac, and Michigan Territory, a confusion of names brought about by the changes of possession and titles used by the French, English and Americans, as each claimed possession.

"Province" was preferred by the French, and "Territory" by the English and Americans. It is most difficult to follow meager reports made by careless officials, and to differentiate correctly, as so many decisions were made by officials instead of governments because of the great isolation of the entire Inner Empire of Ottawa Land.

Chapter Five

Michilimackinac Territory Becomes Michigan Territory

The Straits country was yet to be won, and it was not until 1815 that this was to be a reality. The War of 1812, generally considered to have been brought about by the impressing of American seamen by the British, was in fact much more truly a war to settle differences in the Territory of Michilimackinac. We had come to a realization that this was a part of our country that was well worth fighting for.

Treaties had little effect upon this isolated country, but great was the influence of such men as John Jacob Astor, now becoming rich from his operations in the Straits region, where his company was known as The John Jacob Astor Fur Co., later to become The Great American Fur Co. Robert Morris, who, it was said, had largely financed the Revolution, was a staunch friend of Astor's and his influence bore more weight than all the treaties put together, and the Americans set out once

When Michigan Was Young

more to capture their own in the great northwest.

Meantime, down in Detroit, much progress had been made toward the building of a city, and many settlers had arrived. Many of these people were of the peasant classes of the French, thrifty and anxious to establish permanent homes in the new world. An interesting feature of their settlement was that their farms were all long and narrow, each home bordering on the Detroit River, with the houses near enough to each other for mutual protection. The farm lands stretched back like long lanes to the end of each man's claim, and farm work was done in groups under armed guards. So to this day Detroit's streets, running back from the river, bear the names of that city's first residents while the names of their children appear on the old cross streets.

General William Hull of Massachusetts, in charge of the garrison, knew nothing of frontier life, nor did he understand the French. He was not a man of strong character, was apt to discount the sound advice of wiser men. It was against such advice from Lewis Cass, a brilliant lawyer, and Judge Woodward and others, that Hull, with little resistance, surrendered the fort at Detroit to the English. George B. Catlin, a Michigan historian, says, "The American flag was ingloriously hauled down and again the blooded banner of England flew from the flagstaff after an interval of fifteen years of American possession."

Charges were later laid against Hull by Lewis Cass, and the former was tried by court martial and convicted, but he was never punished.

Not until the victory of Oliver Hazard Perry in the Battle of Lake Erie, September 10, 1813, was Michigan returned to American possession. Detroit was repossessed in that same September, but Fort Mackinac was still

Michilimackinac Territory Becomes Michigan Territory

held by the British until 1815.

Upon repossession of the fort at Detroit, renamed Fort Shelby, life in the settlement took on some degree of peace for the Americans, mostly of French descent.

However, matters were not to be settled entirely until after Tecumseh, another ambitious and rather clever Indian, had caused some trouble with a series of raids which came near ruining things again. But Tecumseh was not as shrewd as Pontiac and failed in his attempts to arouse enough followers to overthrow the American government again.

Lewis Cass, now territorial governor, was gaining influence in Washington and succeeded in bringing the Congress to a full realization of the fact that the Federal government must place itself back of the Detroiters and the rest of the Michilimackinac country in more than a casual way. A commission consisting of a governor and three judges was appointed and sent into what was now termed Michigan Territory to set up a sort of colonial government. The territory was divided into three parts, with counties separated from each other in political units. It was now called the Territory of Michigan by official act of Congress.

This arrangement worked very well for a time. The period is known as the reign of the governors and judges and is looked upon almost as a matter of amusement in Michigan's history, for the people mostly governed themselves. Rather, they were inclined to dictate to the governors. They were definitely in a mood for statehood.

The history of the Territory of Michigan is unique in the fact that for nearly a half century Detroit and its surrounding regions considered themselves the Territory, with scant consideration for the upper part of the peninsula. As a matter of fact, had it not been for its being a

When Michigan Was Young

peninsula, probably there would never have been a State of Michigan, for as state after state was clipped off the old Territory, each in turn trespassed on Michigan's territorial toes until it was indeed only a peninsula, and that would not have been left to itself had not swamps bordered its southern boundaries to such an extent that it was almost an island.

When mutterings of war began to be heard in 1812, the British stationed on the Island of St. Joseph under the command of Captain Charles Roberts were ordered to proceed at once to Mackinac Island and capture the fort. Their approach with a force of several hundred soldiers and a thousand Indians was a complete surprise to the American forces under Lieut. Porter Hanks, and since his small garrison of about three hundred men had no chance whatever to protect themselves, Lieut. Hanks wisely surrendered.

This is known as the Battle of British Landing and this name is still applied to the spot on the north side of the island where the English forces made their landing in 1812. There had not been a real shooting battle because of the immediate surrender of the American forces to protect the inhabitants of the island and the small garrison at the fort. But two years later in 1814 what was known as the Battle of Michilimackinac Island did take place at a lookout several hundred feet back of the fort. Again the Americans were defeated by the British, and Major Andrew Holmes of the American forces was killed. The name Fort Holmes was given to the lookout, which in recent years has been substantially rebuilt into a sizable blockhouse still known by that name as a memorial to the brave young American officer who lost his life attempting to defend the spot with a small force of soldiers.

Michilimackinac Territory Becomes Michigan Territory

All of this took place after the treaty of 1783 when the entire Territory of Michilimackinac had been ceded to the United States by the English. However, the latter held their ground at Mackinac until 1815 when the Treaty of Ghent had been signed and proclaimed by both warring parties. And so the Straits country went quietly on its way again with its fish and its furs for several more decades of peace. It was not until shortly before the Civil War, some years after Michigan had become a State, that the Detroit region began to realize that there was also an upper part to the peninsula. This was perhaps just as well for that part of the state for it was providentially kept out of the frontier wranglings and intrigues that were going on in the lower country.

During these years in southern Michigan Territory, Lewis Cass was growing in political stature. Following the governors and judges era, Cass did a splendid job for several years as territorial governor, more than doubling the territory's population and procuring numerous concessions from the Federal Government. But no effort on his part could procure statehood for Michigan. The new Democratic president, Andrew Jackson, wanted to appoint Cass his Secretary of War and so in 1830 John M. Mason, a Kentucky lawyer, was made secretary to Cass and moved to Detroit with his family. The plan was to groom Mason to become governor of the territory and release Lewis Cass for the secretaryship at Washington. Mason was a Virginian, with all the old conservative ideas of that colonial state, and he hated politics. He had been compelled to accept the position offered him by Jackson because of financial needs, but he had no taste for it. His son, Stevens T. Mason, a remarkably brilliant boy of nineteen, acted as his secretary. Cass was in Washington most of the time and the two Masons virtually

When Michigan Was Young

ran the territory. Finally John T. grew restless and at last persuaded Jackson to permit him to retire in favor of his young son Stevens, known to his family as Tom.

In 1831 Lewis Cass became Secretary of War, and John M. Mason shook the dust of Detroit off his feet and cut the entire political mess, and presently the Territory of Michigan found itself entirely under the guidance of Stevens Thomson Mason, a youth of twenty-two, as territorial governor. Though known as the "Boy Governor," young Mason did a man-sized job both as territorial governor and later as governor of the state, for he proceeded at once to lay his plans carefully for the eventual statehood of the territory. But it was uphill work.

There had been a commission sent out from Washington to investigate the claims of Michigan, and its report was to the effect that the territory was all one great bog, altogether too swampy to ever hope to be made into good farming land. Their advice was to let it alone as it was, which was in a way somewhat similar to the situation of Alaska today, for its distance from Washington at that time was fully as great, owing to the round-about journey by way of New York, and its isolation even greater owing to difficult travel. The Territory had one representative in Congress and no vote, and no school or road bounty. And so Governor Mason set out to remedy these evils by starting road building and creating a public school system, and setting up plans for a state university.

Chapter Six

The State of Michigan Enters the Union, 1837

About the time Michigan Territory got set to become a State, a controversy arose over a small corner of land claimed by both Ohio and Michigan Territory. The village of Toledo happened to be in this strip of land and it decidedly preferred to be a part of a state than a part of a territory; so the two fell into a real frontier wrangle to be known later as the Toledo War, though there had been no blood shed on either side. However, it did convince Washington at last that something really had to be done to placate the two warring factions. Lewis Cass had gone on from Secretary of War to Minister to France and had become one of the country's leading statesmen.

Some years prior to this controversy, while Cass was still in Michigan as territorial governor, he had taken a trip up the lakes and had seen for himself something of the vast mineral deposits in what is now the Upper Peninsula of Michigan. One thing in particular had impressed him deeply, and that was the great copper boulder that is now in the Smithsonian Museum at Washington, D. C. So now, with Lucius Lyon, territorial senator, working vigorously for statehood, and Stevens T. Mason leaving no effort undone for the cause, the time seemed ripe for action. Between them Washington finally settled down for the consideration of Michigan's cause. The result was that if Michigan would consent to allow Ohio to have its small strip of land, what is now the Upper Peninsula of Michigan would be taken away from Wisconsin and given to Michigan.

Martin Van Buren had come into the White House in 1837 to find affairs pretty badly mixed up after Jackson's last administration, and found himself forced to palacate first one and then another political faction. One of his means was to bring several new states in the Union. It was Michigan's good luck to be one of the favored states, and the surrender of the Ohio strip was done with alacrity, although the annexation of all of that wild land up north was not relished greatly by most of the Detroit leaders. It seemed to them a worthless country, and that it would probably be just a big burden to the rest of the state. In that they were amazingly short-sighted, for the Upper Peninsula has proven itself to be the biggest plum ever dropped in the lap of Michigan, with its great stores of minerals and many other natural resources.

At last Michigan Territory, that great Inner Empire of the Ottawas that had given so many states to the nation, was admitted to the Union as a State in 1837, two hundred and three years after the discovery of the Straits of Michilimackinac by Jean Nicolet and his little group of seven fearless voyageurs who had been sent into the west by Samuel de Champlain to find the China Sea.

Stevens Thomson Mason, the "Boy Governor" of the Territory of Michigan, was promptly elected the first

The State of Michigan Enters the Union, 1837

governor of the State of Michigan, and served it faithfully until through political intrigue and wire-pulling the Whigs took over and the political career of Mason was suddenly ended.

Governor Mason had made John D. Pierce superintendent of public instruction to open the way for the splendid educational system of the present day. A grant of land had been obtained for the University of Michigan, and plans were well under way for its start. Highways and railroads were in contemplation, and the governor also had a hazy dream of locks to be constructed at Sault St. Marie in the years to come. Young Governor Mason was a man of great vision. Born in Virginia, and Kentucky raised, he was a sincere and tireless Michigan booster. His death a few years after his departure from Detroit to live in New York, closed a colorful chapter in the historic past of Michigan. In 1905 his remains were returned to Detroit and interred in that city with great pomp and ceremony in a small park set aside for that honor, and a statue of the first governor of the State of Michigan was placed above it.

As Michigan came into its own as a State it seemed fitting that a state seal be designated, and no more capable man than Lewis Cass could have been chosen to suggest the principal features of the design. In this recital of Michigan's story so far, the aboriginal owners of Michigan seem to have been forgotten, a fact done with intent because their story will be told in its own way in other stories. But Lewis Cass had not forgotten the part the Ottawa nation had played in securing final peace, and the refusal of many of them to enter into the ferocious plans of Pontiac. So he designated the Michigan State Seal with a moose, the totem crest of the Ottawa nation on one side of the banner, and an elk on the other side.

When Michigan Was Young

For the motto he chose to paraphrase the motto placed on an entrance to Westminster Abbey by Sir Christopher Wren, "If you seek a beautiful structure look about you," changing the motto to read "If you seek a beautiful Peninsula, look about you."

Not until 1911 was this seal produced correctly, or nearly so. It has been a source of no end of discussions in the legislature. Every artist asked to copy it has taken liberties in the design. One even put manes on the animals. None of them stuck entirely to the original design.

The fascinating story of Mackinac Island has been told by many historians. It is now the summer home of Michigan's governors, and of many hundreds of other summer residents and tourists. Its Grand Hotel is perhaps the largest resort hotel in the world. From the time hundreds of years ago when the Ottawas looked upon the Fairy Isle as a sacred spot it has been a place apart from the rest of the country about it. Sitting serenely at the northern end of the Straits of Mackinac, it guards the passage from Lake Superior to the lower lakes of the inland group and keeps to itself its part of the story of Michigan's historic past — a past when two nations kept their flags unfurled over its picturesque rocks and hills; a past when great fortunes were made in the fur trade, and in its fishing fleets. Mackinac Island's past is so unique that it can be told only in a story by itself.

We have watched the invasion of the forests by the white race. We have witnessed the subjugation of the aboriginal peoples by the white man as a part of the march of civilization, and we have learned of the intensive struggle of the invaders to broaden their own and the lives of the natives of the land. A further study would tell us that the original inhabitants of Michigan have become almost completely absorbed into the life of

The State of Michigan Enters the Union, 1837

the state. So much so that in a Michigan school a short time ago when a class was asked to state in writing in as few words as possible who were the first Americans, an Ottawa Indian boy wrote simply "I am," and signed his name.

Only recently a state publication reported that the Indian population of Detroit, the state's principal city, is numbered at one thousand people, and it is more than probable that as many more of mixed blood are to be found there alone. All over the state there are scattered groups and villages of Indians leading lives far removed from the desperate extremities of their ancestors.

Within the past year a group of Indians calling themselves Chippewas, living on what had been one of the last government reservations in Michigan was released from their last government restraint in connection with the sale of their lands. There are about five hundred of these people who were once a part of the ancient Ojibway nation. Until a few years ago a government school was maintained for them in the heart of the old reservation in Isabella County. It is said that at one time there were Indians in this school from forty-five tribes, including two boys from the Seneca nation.

It is no uncommon thing to find descendants of both eastern and western Indian nations living today among the Ottawas and Ojibways of Michigan in perfect amity.

In considering these aboriginal peoples one must alsays take into account the fact that the nation was the great parent body, the tribe a divisional body. Transportation was slow, either by canoe, pony, or foot trail. This necessitated the establishment of thousands of villages, and as soon as a village became a reality a name was created for it, and it soon became known as a tribe. These tribes lived almost entirely according to their rulings under the guidance of their chosen councilmen and chiefs.

A complicated system of signals and runners kept these chains of villages informed of events of high import to all. In time of war, or the hostile approach of enemies, the system sprang to life, and in surprisingly short time the entire chain of tribes, spread over hundreds of thousands of acres of land, was able to come together as a nation. Much confusion has resulted with the acceptance of tribal names as those of nations. Records and treaties were not too carefully worded in the pioneer days of the United States, and the founding of our nation.

Michigan's Indians are a valued part of the state's life today, with both men and women given their voting franchise. Michigan's evolution from a vast aboriginal Inner Empire through its years as a French Province, a great Territorial area of the United States from which most of the Middle Western states were separated, to its present position of prestige among the states of the nation in a little over three hundred years since its discovery by Jean Nicolet in 1634, forms one of the most interesting and most important of the epics of our national history.

PART II

ANCIENT GUARDIANS OF THE STRAITS OF MICHILIMACKINAC

Chapter Seven

Nicolet Discovers the Straits of Michilimackinac

The third centenary of the discovery of the Straits of Michilimackinac and the establishment of that locality as a strategic and commercial center occurred in August in the year 1934. The honor of this great discovery must be given to the young French courier de bois, Jean Nicolet, commissioned by Champlain to find the western passage to India and China, but destined by fate to become one of the world's great explorers and the father of commerce in that vast territory which soon came to be known as the Province of Michilimackinac.

One hundred years before the arrival of Nicolet in the Straits country, Jacques Cartier, a vice admiral of France, had sailed into the Bay of Gaspe off the coast of Newfoundland and planted the colors of France, calling the land New France in America. During the century that followed, fishing and fur trading flourished in the new world, and forts for the protection of traders and voyageurs had been established. Cartier's discovery of the mouth of the St. Lawrence River in 1534 had opened a way into the interior of the country, but little advancement had been made until the year 1608 when Samuel de Champlain founded the fort and city of Quebec eight hundred miles from the ocean.

Champlain himself had ventured into the mysterious Indian countries of the west as early as 1610 with a company of sixty warriors, only a few of whom he dared entrust with muskets. The expedition was not a success, its only notable result being the introduction to the Indians of the lakes of "weapons of war that spoke noise and fire and death." Champlain had been told by the Indians that the country of the big lakes was filled with fur-bearing animals, that fish were always plentiful, and that copper could be found in abundance. They had also told him that fear of the deadly Iroquois prevented their venturing far into this region of wealth and wide waters. It was more than twenty years after his own failure to penetrate the west that Champlain found a man capable of leading another expedition westward in search of the coveted passage to India and China, the urge that had sent Columbus out on the high seas, and had sent Jacques Cartier in 1534 to the fishing banks of Newfoundland.

Jean Nicolet had come to New France as a boy of eighteen in search of the thrills of a new land. He possessed a remarkable gift of dialect comprehension and very soon became a valuable interpreter for the French among the many tribes of Indians along the St. Lawrence. His kindly, lovable nature, and perfect fearlessness, with an invariable sense of justice, establish him among the Indians as a friend. He lived alone for a number of years in an isolated spot on Lake Superior in charge of a trading outpost. His

Nicolet Discovers the Straits of Michilimackinac

surroundings were most unwholesome and his privations were many; at one time he subsisted for weeks, with his Indian companions, on the bark of trees as their only food. His historians tell us that strength, courage, and a great beauty of character were his inheritance from these years of conflict with the life of the frontier. It was in this spirit that Nicolet set out on his great quest. The uncharted beyond was his goal; the realities, when known, his prize. Whatever these might be the high purpose of the man was equal to the encounter. Like Champlain, his dream was all for the glory of France and her prestige in the discovery of the long-sought western passage.

But unlike Champlain who had been dominated by superior officers who sought only for gain as traders, and consequently had been hampered in his desire for exploring the western country, Nicolet instead was urged to his undertaking by Champlain, who had meantime become commandant at Fort Quebec and director in New France of the rapidly growing fur business, as representative of the One Hundred Associates in France.

A man now in his early thirties, Nicolet still retained the Frenchman's love of the dramatic. Fleet Indian runners were sent in advance to the villages of the Indian nations bordering the route of the party to announce its approaching arrival in the region of the western waters, and altogether the expediton took on a tone of grandeur and display. Preparations for the trip had consumed a period of many months, and several more were required for the difficult voyage of Nicolet and his little band of seven followers in their dugout canoes, to traverse the route from the trading station on the St. Lawrence river to the Straits. It is historically certain that a stop was made at Mackinac Island; but where Nicolet really held this first conference between white men and Indians in the region of the Straits is most indefinite. It seems probable that it took place not far from the present city of St. Ignace in an ancient Indian village, as a stop was recorded as having been made there. Many names have been given to this historic spot, but the French designation of the place as Iroquois Pointe seems to have been the most popular and permanent.

It was no doubt in deference to the desires of the student element of France that Nicolet presented himself to the Indians in the gorgeous robes of a Chinese Mandarin; the object of this, of course, being to arouse a remembrance in the minds of the Indians of their supposed origin. A more dramatic scene could hardly be imagined.

Large bands of warriors had assembled to welcome this strange messenger and his friends to the country of the Indians of the Lakes. War bonnets and painted faces must have been their brave adornment, and tomahawks their weapons; while Jean Nicolet, perhaps the bravest man at the moment on the American continent, with his little band of seven white men, stood among them in his brilliant Chinese robes holding high above his head two huge pistols. As he approached the assemblage he shot them both into the air.

It was fortunate for Nicolet that the great host of painted warriors received him hospitably and gladly accepted his message of peace. Nicolet was happily accepted by the Indians and his position was at once established among them as that of a friend, and the quantities of gifts that he had brought were graciously received.

The splendid diplomacy of Nicolet in the conference that followed undoubtedly laid the foundation for the extensive trading operations and future colonizations of the

Nicolet Discovers the Straits of Michilimackinac

French in the great Province of Michilimackinac, for the pipe of peace was smoked at this gathering, and a complete understanding was arranged with the result that the Michilimackinac region shortly became a part of New France. At this time, too, there was erased the age-old myth of a westward flowing river leading to India and China, for the Indian's descriptions of the western lands effaced further thought of such a thing.

The result of the conference, or treaty, was the claim of France to "all lands bordering on the inland seas and lying westward of them." Just how big a bite the French were taking in this was most uncertain, as Spain already laid claim to much of this same unknown country. To protect the claim of the French, however, as soon as possible a rude stockade fort was established on the Straits. This first stronghold of the white man in the region of the Straits was located on Iroquois Pointe, not far from St. Ignace, near the little Indian village called Taenhotentaron. The date of the arrival of the first garrison is uncertain, but it was probably several years after the conference.

Chapter Eight

The First Guardian of the Straits

The first military stockade in the Michilimackinac country was called Fort de Buade in honor of Louis de Buade, Comte de Frontenac, at that time hero of the wars in Holland, and native of Nicolet's home locality in France, but later to become governor of Canada in New France. The exact date of the establishment of this fort is not historically positive. A garrison of two hundred soldiers was eventually sent to the new fort by the commandant at Quebec, and a thriving fur trading station was set up to control the output of the tribes living about the Straits. The fur trading post of Michilimackinac on Iroquois Pointe soon became the base of supplies for the entire northwest and the center of the fur trade of the Province of Michilimackinac. An encampment of nearly one thousand allied Indian warriors on the Pointe added to the security of Fort De Buade.

Whether a fort was maintained continuously at Pointe Iroquois during the half century that followed is quite uncertain. Baron La Hontan, in 1688, made mention in

When Michigan Was Young

his Relations of the settlement in the following words: "Michilimackinac is situated very advantageously, for the Iroquese dare not venture, with their sorrie canoes, to cross the Straits of the Illinese Lake, which is two leagues over; besides that the Lake of the Hurons is too rough for such slender boats, and as they cannot come by water, so they cannot approach by land by reason of the marshes, fens, and little rivers which it would be very difficult to cross, not to mention that the Straits of the Illinese Lake lies still in their way."

And so we know that some sort of a post was entrenched on the northern side of the Straits in 1688. Evidently La Hontan did not know that a general exodus of Ojibways of La Pointe du Saint Esprit far to the north was even then being planned, and was to be led by the mighty Indian Chief Wabojeeg to a new home in the Michilimackinac province. The terror of the deadly Iroquois, ever on the warpath, and encroaching farther and farther westward from their homeland east of the Alleghanies, was now driving nation after nation to the protection of the friendly tribes. In more ways than one it was to be a momentous one for Michilimackinac province. Pere Marquette, spiritual guide of these people at the Mission of Saint Esprit, Sault Ste. Marie, followed them into the new country, and during the winter of 1669 and 1670 he lived on the Island of Mackinac, where another trading post was now established, while building his mission near Fort De Buade on Pointe Iroquois four miles to the north.

And to the halfbreed Indian wife of Schoolcraft, the historian, who was proud of the fact that she was the granddaughter of the Great Chief Wabojeeg, we are indebted for the wonderful stories and legends relating to her people, the Chippewas, or Ojibways, that have come to us in the writings of her husband and numerous other

The First Guardian of the Straits

friends to whom she loved to tell them.

Much confusion has existed regarding the names of the various settlements about the Straits in ancient times. If one learns to differentiate between the military posts and the trading posts the mystery is at once cleared. At the start one must realize that the two identities were absolutely separate, although of necessity they moved from one place to another together as a matter of protection. Then, too, one must realize that in reports going back to France leaders of both military posts and commercial posts quite naturally assumed the role of greatest importance in the new country.

In the military archives of France Fort De Buade, garrisoned by soldiers courageous enough to guard this extreme outpost of civilization among savage tribes, no doubt stood as the dominant factor in the new region.

On the other hand, the great fur trading post of Michilimackinac, through which passed annually thousands and thousands of rich fur pelts for the markets of Europe, also took to itself the prestige of dominating the locality in name at least; and the entire Straits region became known soon after its settlement as "Michilimackinac," whether the term meant one place or another on the Straits. At so great a distance, in a time when leagues determined thought, this was not in the least strange.

It is for us today to endeavor to untangle this history and legend as carefully as possible in an effort to be of some slight service to future historical writers, and to the thousands of interested travelers who pass through this wonderful region of the Straits each year.

As other settlements sprang up about the Straits, the one on Pointe Iroquois became known as "North Michilimackinac," and so it remained for many years.

Sometime about the middle of the seventeenth century

When Michigan Was Young

there was a terrible massacre by the Iroquois and Huron tribes at Pointe Iroquois. Ottawas, Ojibways, and other allies of the French scattered in all directions, to the Isle de Castor, the Manitoulins, Michilimackinac and other islands, and even as far south as the lower end of the Lake of the Illinese. As no one would go to the Pointe to trade after that, for several years the place was deserted, even the stockade fort being closed for a time, until the scare was over and the former allies began to return, well knowing that they would receive gifts and rum for their furs.

There were many changes of command, no one remaining long on the job. There is record that one de la Porc Louvigny was commandant at Michilimackinac and its dependencies for some years prior to the arrival of La Mothe de la Cadillac in 1694. About this time the French court decided that it could not afford to garrison so many forts in its Inner Empire and ordered many of them closed. Fort De Buade at Michilimackinac and St. Joseph to the south end of the Illinese Lake remained manned, however. Commandant Frontenac, now at Fort Frontenac at Kingston on the St. Lawrence disagreed with this order. Since the weighty decisions of the French court required a long time for debate, and transportation of letters covered many months and often even years, it is believed that Frontenac simply went on as usual and no doubt reports sent back to France did not fully cover the facts. Frontenac knew that the traders must be protected, else they would be completely stranded in this hostile land, and that many lives would be sacrificed, and that he was not willing to face. So the forts remained manned until full reports could be considered and the objectionable orders could be withdrawn.

In the person of Cadillac, there appeared for the first

The First Guardian of the Straits

time in the great trading center of Michilimackinac, the true pioneer spirit, the ambition of a real colonist. Cadillac dreamed of the establishment of a new military power in the Inner Empire of Michilimackinac province; of a civilization surrounding it that might eventually rival that of the Old World. But many of his ideas did not coincide with those of the mission fathers, and there were now many of these zealous men in the Michilimackinac country.

Cadillac was altogether too liberal with his distribution of "fire-water" among the Indians. He was an impatient man, wanted things done quickly, and this seemed the quickest means to his ends. The upshot was that Cadillac decided to found a settlement of his own, with a fort at his command. Though it took several years to accomplish his design, and a stay of some time in France, he finally obtained consent from the king to start a colony at the lower end of the lake at a place called De Troit. He called his new Fort Ponchartrain, and his village Detroit.

During his absence in France Lieutenant Louvigny was in command of Fort de Buade, and when Cadillac finally left his Straits country for good in 1701 to move his garrison to Fort Ponchartrain, Louvigny was left in charge of a small garrison and what was left of the trading center that had controlled commerce in the great Inner Empire for more than a century and a half.

Though Cadillac was joined in his new venture by several hundred Indians of various small tribes, it is a notable fact that the Ottawas, in this year, asked their "French Father to prohibit the gift of strong drink among their people." This was, no doubt, at the instigation of the missionaries, as the Ottawas had received the priests from Fort De Buade and its near villages at La Croix, in the Arbre Croche region, when Cadillac dismantled the fort.

When Michigan Was Young

Louvigny must have remained in the region, and must have had at least a small group of soldiers with him for some years, for we learn that he "was the first Commandant at New Michilimackinac," and that was located at Pointe Pequotenance on the southern shore of the Straits, right in the heart of the Ojibway camp where La Salle had located a trading post in 1668. The little garrison was given recognition by the French court in 1712, with Lieutenant Louvigny still in charge as its first commandant.

The commercial and military life of Michilimackinac had come a long way since 1634 when Jean Nicolet first set foot on the soil of the future state of Michigan. Seventy-eight years had passed. Crowded with events of supreme importance, these years had witnessed many changes. From the desire to conquer and to trade, the desire now had become one of empire, not for the Ottawas and Ojibways, the aborigines of the land, but for the French in the land of New France. At the same time the English had worked their way up from the eastern seaboard in what we now call the New England States, and down from the shores of Newfoundland, which they had captured, and the Hudson's Bay country, to what the French had begun to call Canada, and were crowding down into the Straits country. Both the Northwest Passage and the Western Passage to the China Sea had been abandoned for the more lucrative business of hunting the beaver and other wild animals for their valuable fur.

Chapter Nine

Fort Michilimackinac

During all these years trading posts, forts, and missions moved in more or less unison with each other from one advantageous place to another. The trading posts supplied the commercial incentive, while the forts put the fear of man in the hearts of the Indians and supplied the legal balance between the many traders and the Indians. The missions with their limited personnel did all they could to inject moral concepts into the entire outfit. It has been reported that several thousand priests came to New France in the course of the two first centuries after its discovery by Cartier. No more tragic or heroic chapter could possibly be written than the story of the suffering and martyrdom of hundreds of these young priests.

We have passed a turning point in the history of the Straits of Michilimackinac with the establishment of a new military base on the southern, or mainland, shore of the Straits. Because of the destruction of the first Fort de Buade, a reoccupancy of that base must have necessitated the building of a second fort. So this new fort can be considered the third to be built in the Straits locality.

They were all built more or less in a similar manner. There would be a center space for cabins and a well built stockade of pickets, usually about twenty feet long, set deep in the ground and placed close together. The cabins in Fort de Buade numbered about sixty, according to La Hontan. Two rows of pickets were usually set up with a space of some ten or more feet between them, and this space would be filled with rocks and sand and all sorts of rubble to form a wall. Heavy gates, or doors, with massive iron hinges and locking bars, protected the entrances. In the very early years only the most trusted Indian allies were permitted to carry muskets. There were two hundred well drilled and equipped soldiers at Fort De Buade when La Hontan visited it in 1688. Small "lookouts" or solidly built block-houses, perched at intervals above the crude rubble walls, were always manned with soldiers ever on the lookout for mauraders. We may well imagine that a stray arrow deftly shot often flew over these crude ramparts to create shock and disaster.

It is almost impossible to believe in our day that a structure of this sort could have been considered "A fine fort," as La Hontan described Fort De Buade in 1688.

The name De Buade did not carry over from North Michilimackinac to South Michilimackinac, which became known at once as Fort Michilimackinac. The southern fort was under the command of Lieutenant Louvigny for some years after 1712. The garrison was still maintained with about two hundred troops, and the trading went on as it had on the north shore, while the missions were set up at La Croix, several miles to the south around Pointe Teangabing.

With the removal of Cadillac to the new Fort Poncha-

Stone monument marking the site of Fort Michilimackinac where almost the entire English garrison was massacred in the Pontiac Conspiracy of 1763

Fort Michilimackinac

train at De Troit, so much of the fur trading left the Straits country and so many Indians followed Cadillac to the new location that little attention was paid to what was going on in the Straits country. But this lasted only a few years. Again the missionaries and Cadillac were not in accord, and many of the Indians began to drift back to their old homes in the Straits country. The Inner Empire had lost its tranquil life, a sort of pulling and hauling had taken its place. By 1714 Father Marest was pleading with the king of France to reestablish the Garrison at De Buade, and so we find a protective establishment of sorts at Pointe Iroquois in 1721, when Father Charlevoix paid the place a visit and reported that "there is here now only a middling village because of the dispersement of the Indians to the lower Fort and the islands of the Lakes." However, he continued to say that "many Indians still bring their peltries to this station because it is the passage or meeting place of many nations in the lake countries." It evidently was still, as it had always been, the neutral meeting place of the lake tribes.

And so it seems quite probable that there were both trading posts and garrisons at the north and at the south at the same time for some years. While Champlain had ordered his life and the affairs of his command strictly according to the dictates of the French court, often to his own dire confusion, his followers at both Quebec and Frontenac, now commanding under far different circumstances, were obliged to act with greater rapidity and hence to follow their own dictates of common sense, and it is more than probable that as a consequence reports of just what happened and what didn't very often went back to France somewhat different than the facts in New France would seem to have taken place. As in our own day it must have been most difficult for the French court to see eye to eye with the progress of the life in New France. And there must always be considered in the life of those times the extreme slowness of transportation. Decisions of any sort took many months and often years for debate and fulfillment. The Inner Empire was more or less a kingdom ruled over by commandants, traders, and priests. It is not surprising that there were many conflicts of will.

From the date of Cadillac's departure from Fort De Buade in 1701, commanding officers came and went at both North and South Michilimackinac with frequency, almost as if small groups of soldiers were sent to these western outposts as a matter of change in their monotonous lives in the larger forts on the St. Lawrence. And the British continued to entice the Indians to their trading posts in Canada with their peltries with the promise of higher prices and more rum, and incitations of belligerence to French rulings. These dissensions continued until with the fall of Quebec in September, 1759, and with the subsequent surrender of New France in 1763 to the British, everything changed in the Inner Empire.

The Indians mostly preferred the French, who lived like brothers in their camps, gave them many presents, and in so many instances affiliated with their tribes and married their maidens. They were never able to understand the aloofness of the English, who seldom came to live in their teepees permanently, and who gave very few presents. They felt that they were not with masters, but equals among the French, while the English treated them "like dogs" and dealt with them only when it was necessary for trading purposes. These were the things that formed the background for the great Pontiac Massacre.

By 1760 Fort Michilimackinac, under English command, was one of the strongest outposts in Michili-

Fort Michilimackinac

mackinac province. In 1763 we find Captain George Etherington in command of the fort, and since hostilities had quieted down to a certain degree of safety, numerous trading posts were scattered about the peninsula of L'Arbre Croche, with the little mission churches always settled within easy access to the fort or posts.

The Arbre Croche locality was definitely an Ottawa center. Their capital village of Wagonokezee was located on the shores of La Petite Traverse, the "little crossing," a body of water lying east of Lake Michilimackinac to form the small peninsula. They were becoming a pastoral people in this sylvan retreat, and they liked the quiet life, away from the fighting and wrangling of the other nations. That is why, perhaps, that it began to be noticed that they were becoming inclined to favor the English, who, whey must have noted, did endeavor to live at peace in their camps about the Straits, and particularly on Mackinac Island, where they had centered with their families and their trading. And so the Ottawas, for one reason or another, did not enter into the Pontiac Conspiracy, to their everlasting honor. The story of Alexander Henry, one of the few survivors of the massacre of Fort Pequotenonce, most graphically tells the terrible tale of this disaster, and of the manner in which his life was saved by these friendly Ottawas of L'Arbre Croche.

The story of the Pontiac raid is too harrowing for this recital, which is supposed to place before the reader the names, locations and numbers of forts located about the Straits of Michilimackinac prior to the formation of Michigan as a state; and also to give some slight knowledge of their formation and other details deemed essential to an understanding of the struggles endured by the white pioneers of the Inner Empire, and the limitations

When Michigan Was Young

under which they lived. We must always bear in mind that trading posts, with forts to protect them and missions to give them a gleam of civilization, formed the basis of life and the entering wedges of progress from the old world to the revolutionization of the Inner Empire of the savage of the west to the ways of life of the east.

After the failure of the Pontiac Conspiracy in 1763 to wrest the entire Inner Empire from the English, much larger forces were sent into the country in an attempt to hold what had been won from the French, and a second fort was built at Pequotenonce to replace the one demolished by the Pontiac forces. A Michigan state park is now located on the site of this ancient fort. A replica of the last fort on this spot has been built and on a great boulder monument a large bronze plate has been placed that fully describes this most tragic occurrence of the Strait's history. The inscription reads as follows:

"On this site was situated Fort Michilimackinac. The site became known as 'Old Mackinac' after the removal of the Fort to Mackinac Island in 1781. The Indian name of the site was Pequotenonce meaning headland or bluff. The Fort was transferred to this site some time after 1712, was held by the French until 1760, was garrisoned by the English in 1761 under Captain George Etherington. As a part of the conspiracy of Pontiac against the English, June 4, 1763, the Ojibways under Chief Minavavana captured the fort and massacred nearly the entire garrison."

The place is now called Wawatam Park, a Michilimackinac state tourist park, honoring the Ottawa chief whom tradition declares to have rescued several of the white inhabitants of the fort. It is one of the most beautiful parks in Northern Michigan, and thousands of tourists find the spot a delightful camping ground.

Chapter Ten

The British Appear in Michilimackinac

From the beginning of the settlements of the French and English on the Atlantic Coast there had been rivalry for the favor of the Indians because of the fur trade. As this trade developed a serious factor arose in the difference between trading prices in the two groups. The English could supply blankets, clothing and rum much cheaper than could the French, owing to the fact that the former could send their ships back and forth across the ocean more often because landings could be made in the ports bordering on the lower country being colonized by the English the year around, while the French could not make as many trips because of the colder weather and ice-closed ports along the St. Lawrence. Also there were continual encroachments upon the other's claimed territory by adherents of both nations.

This struggle went on for more than a hundred years, while the Five Nations headed by the Iroquois stood between them like a great human wall which neither group dared to invade.

It was Sir William Johnson, the famous Indian agent of the English, who discerned the fact that the real key to the French trading stations of the west was the military base on the Straits, and as a consequence, with the aid of Brant, his Indian ally, Johnson was ever fomenting disturbances among the French and the Indians of the lake country. His was the real force behind the French and Indian War, and it was his cruelty and cunning that made the contest such a tragedy.

It was during this war that silver medals of various sizes were given by the English to the chiefs of their allied tribes for their valor in battle. A number of these medals are still owned in the Mackinac country. The medals bear the coat of arms of England on one side, while on the reverse appears, in bold relief, the head and bust of George III of England. On the breast of the king, just above the heart, may be seen the head of an Indian chief, the whole representing the Indians as children of the king resting within his heart in perfect safety.

Fort Michilimackinac, on the site of the Pontiac massacre, was re-established by the English in 1765. The new fort was built of several rows of heavy timbers forming a stockade. Several feet of space were allowed between these rows, and massive timbers, set deep in the ground, stood some thirty feet above the ground on the outer row. Two companies of troops under Captain Howard formed the garrison at the time of reoccupation. This was the fourth fort to guard the Straits of Michilimackinac.

Intimations have been found in the Jesuit Relations of a mission during these years on the lower mainland, and the influence of such a mission was found by those who came for religious work in this field at a later date, but records regarding these missions are indefinite. A great

The British Appear in Michilimackinac

cross stands on the bluff at Cross Village at the present time; tradition asserts this cross was erected there many years ago to replace its duplicate which tradition maintains was planted in that spot by Father Marquette while working among the people of the long village of L'Arbre Croche, which encircled the entire point now known as Cross Village Point.

With the coming of the English the Jesuits destroyed their mission at St. Ignace and retired to the province of Quebec, but a parish was eventually established at Mackinac Island and has remained there ever since.

In France the favor of Louis XIV for the English removed many of their problems in America, and so the life of the Straits of Michilimackinac was allowed to move on its way in comparative serenity for nearly thirty years. The trading post was now located on the Island, and thousands of rich fur pelts and hundreds of cargoes of fish were shipped out into the world unheeding almost entirely the great struggle of the American Colonists that was being waged only a few hundred miles away.

Then, from the confusion of the great world in 1770, came sturdy, thrifty, ambitious Captain Patrick Sinclair, of His Majesty's forces, and one-time member of the 42nd Highlanders, or Black Watch Regiment. Captain Sinclair brought into the quiet of the frontier life of Michilimackinac ideas of his own regarding the future neeeds of the Straits region for protection. The dilapidated pickets of the old stockade confounded him, and straightway visions arose in the Scotchman's thrifty mind of an impregnable stronghold somewhere on the Straits in a more advantageous position than he found Fort Michilimackinac to be, situated as it was on the lower mainland where a commanding view of the Straits was impossible. The fairy isle only a few miles across the water at once

Medal given by the English to the chiefs of their allied tribes for their valor in battle against the French in the French and Indian War attracted his attention and enthusiastic reports were forwarded to his commandant at Quebec. Almost before the carrier could reach there, Sinclair wrote again portraying the wonders of the Island as a commanding position for a real fort, for this was now quite clearly in his mind.

The result of Sinclair's vigorous enthusiasm was the building of what was later considered one of the strongest and most perfect forts in America, rivaling the famous fort of Gibralter in its position and possibilities as a stronghold.

The new fort on Mackinac Island was the fifth fort to be built on the Straits of Mackinac, as there had been two built on the south shore at the present Mackinac City. The Island fort would now be the third military base.

The British High Command designated the splendid new stronghold as Fort Michilimackinack, using the final **k**, though Michilimackinac was always spelled by the French without that English **k**.

The treaty made on September 3, 1783, ceding "that part of the French Province of Michilimackinac south of the Great Lakes" to the United States seemed to have no bearing on the situation whatever, except to confuse, for the English calmly remained at the fort for some years. The war worn inhabitants of the east had quite enough trouble at home without seeking it in the northwest, and the English were allowed to remain at Fort George unmolested, carrying on extensive trading in furs and fish with the Indians.

The fort was the pride of Captain Sinclair's heart. He was virtually monarch of all he surveyed during the next few years, for he had also been made civil governor of the Straits region. New France had some time previously been divided into four provinces, with a governor in

The British Appear in Michilimackinac

control of each of them. Boundaries were never clearly defined, but that fact didn't seem to matter as they seldom ever conflicted.

It was truly a glorious time for the Island as many young officers brought their wives and other relatives to the post where a gay social life was maintained. Many of the French fur traders who continued at the Island were members of the finest families of France, and the English officers and soldiers the pick of the English blue bloods. It was but natural then that a high degree of culture and exclusiveness existed in this isolated little military and civic center of civilization in the new world.

Fort Michilimackinack was splendidly built. Nearly all of the heavy hardwood timbers of the old fort were transported across the Straits on the "Welcome," a sturdy sailing vessel used in the fur trade, captained by Alex Harrow, another Scotchman who promptly clashed with Sinclair in regard to authority in the region. Sinclair as usual, was found to be in the right and the affair eventually was settled with satisfaction to all.

The walls of the fort were six feet thick, partly built of rock and mortar, and partly of stout timbers. With three large blockhouses surmounting its walls, it was considered proof against any attack of munitions or arrows. One of the old blockhouses still stands, exactly as it did when its small iron cannon was considered adequate protection against any siege.

It is probable from statistical deductions that the English expended in the building of Fort Michilimackinack nearly, if not quite, an equivalent of what would now be $500,000 American money. It was hardly possible that a certainty prevailed in the English mind at that time that the Treaty of Paris, of 1783, would stand perpetually. Had not the War of 1812 finally settled the matter, the present ownership of Mackinac Island might not have been American. Surrender of Fort Michilimackinack was made to American forces June, 1796. It had been a British stronghold for more than a dozen years, though actually a possession of the United States since the Treaty of 1783.

It will be noted that the Island fort has been alluded to as "Fort George." Officially it was Fort Michilimackinac to the English, but to Sinclair it was always Fort George, as he had wished it to be called in the first place.

Chapter Eleven

American Possession of Fort Mackinac

July 17, 1812, after a period of sixteen years of peace for the Straits, during which time the fort was again called Fort Mackinac, Captain Roberts of the English forces landed with one hundred and fifty soldiers and a thousand Indians at an unprotected spot on the northern shore of the Island. The place is still called "British Landing." Lieutenant Porter Hanks, in command of the garrison of fifty-seven men, wisely preferred immediate surrender by messenger rather than the wholesale massacre that threatened the little settlement. The fort was turned over to the English without bloodshed. A few of the Islanders declared allegiance to Britain, but most of them were sent away with the American soldiers on parole until an exchange of prisoners could be effected.

One more attempt was made by the Americans to recapture the fort prior to its final surrender in 1815. On a date between the 4th and 8th of August, 1814, a company of American soldiers landed on the shores of the Island.

But they had been betrayed by an Indian spy, and the English lay in wait for them about a mile from the fort. Redoubts had been thrown up in the form of strong earthworks around a small blockhouse that it is believed was originally designed by Sinclair as a part of the complete plan of the fort that was later greatly reduced from his plans, and this he had continued to call Fort George. A short but hard fought battle took place on this spot, and Major Andrew Holmes, an American soldier, was killed. Major Holmes was dearly loved by his soldiers and by his friends, and the old blockhouse was always afterward called "Fort Holmes" in his honor after American possession of the Island. It was later used for target practice by the troops stationed at the fort. Finally the building was removed by parts and utilized in the building of stables for the fort, but later sentiment caused the return of the old logs and for many years it remained in its old place. A substantial blockhouse now stands on this eminence which is one of the most sightly on the Island.

The Treaty of Ghent was signed December 24, 1814. It was not proclaimed, however, until February 16, 1815. Formal possession by the Americans, under command of Colonel Anthony Butler, took place on July 18, 1815, when the British finally surrendered "Michilimackinack and all of its Dependencies." Colonel McDonall, with the British forces, retired to Drummond's Island at the mouth of the St. Mary's River, where an English fort was still maintained. Colonel Butler left Captain Willoughby Morgan in command of the fort while he returned to Fort Shelby at Detroit.

The official U.S. Government name for the fort on Mackinac Island has always been "Fort Mackinac," and it is the only one on the Straits over which the flag of the United States has ever floated.

American Possession of Fort Mackinac

All through the one hundred and eighty years of French and English rule in the Straits region the commercial minds of Europe had designated the entire locality as Michilimackinac, if under France and Michilimackinack when under England. It was all one and the same to the great fur dealers on the continent and in England. Names of forts might change, but the general name of the commercial center and location of trading posts was the same, under one name, and always pronounced the same, as if spelled with a 'naw' at the end of the word, no matter which corner of the trading triangle was referred to. It was not until after 1815, when the fort on the island was taken possession of by the Americans, that the three important settlements were properly designated by individual names by Europeans, and Point St. Ignace, Old Mackinac, and Fort Mackinac on Mackinac Island, as Washington designated these various places, became generally accepted.

To the aboriginal claimants of the Inner Empire it had been Missilimokina. The French translated the pronunciation almost correctly, while rendering their own spelling, as the Indians had no written language. The English took the idea literally and insisted upon sounding all the letters and emphasized the final sound with a **k**, and the Americans carelessly permitted the ancient pronunciation to be superseded by the English sound of the last syllable. Mackinac should always be pronounced as was originally intended, "Mackinaw," though spelled Mackinac.

With the departure of the English, Michilimackinac in the region of the Straits soon became known as "The Straits of Mackinac," one of the most important commercial centers in the United States. Colonel Anthony Butler and Major Willoughby Morgan were in command at Fort Mackinac, which gradually became a refuge of rest for the troops from the west where Indian fighting was the order of the day. At a later date troops from the Civil War found rest and health in the salubrious air of the Great Lakes, and it is of record that several Confederate prisoners of high rank were secluded within the walls of the fort for a time, while awaiting exchange of prisoners.

The John Jacob Astor Fur Company, then doing a prosperous business in the lakes country, built a great warehouse on the Island, and a big, rambling, roomy residence house for the company's traders was also erected. The wives and daughters of the officers at the fort, and of the fur company's mangers, were among the most brilliant women of the new Territory of Michilimackinac, and the gay social functions of the Island became the most distinguished affairs of the west, carrying on the traditions of English life in the days of Fort Michilimackinack. Many a romance has been woven about these two dominant factors of the old northwest, the fort and the trading post on the big Island of the inland seas. A thriving village, with churches and schools, sprang up on the Island, and descendants of those "first families" are still to be found living there.

Events ran smoothly for the Island until the departure of the Astor Fur Company from the Straits in 1842. The Astors had grown enormously rich, and the Hudson's Bay Fur Company, reaching down from its stations in the north, coveted the great industry and eventually completely absorbed it under the name of The Great American Fur Company. The once brilliant social center soon slipped back into a little fishing village, and remained so until tourists on steamers of the Great Lakes, soon after the close of the Civil War, discovered the

American Possession of Fort Mackinac

Island's natural beauty and many advantages as a summer resting place.

The removal of the last garrison from Fort Mackinac in 1895 was a source of genuine sadness to the residents of the Island and to the hundreds who were now in the habit of paying annual visits to the spot. The dignity and glamour of military life had given the historic Island an individuality of its own. Visitors still love to ramble about the old walls, inspect the ancient blockhouse, and speculate on the events that took place long ago. The last command at Fort Mackinac was under First Lieutenant E. M. Johnson, Jr., U.S.A., 19th Infantry.

On the 31st day of May, 1895, the military reservation on Mackinac Island, with all its lands and buildings, including grounds set apart prior to this for the purpose of a National Park, was granted to the State of Michigan to be known as "Mackinac Island State Park." Few provisions were attached to the gift to the state from the U.S. Government, the most important being that "The United States Flag is kept floating from the staff of Fort Mackinac under the usual regulations." An added provision plans for the "restoration of the Fort to the United States Government whenever the Secretary of War deems it expedient that such a measure be taken for the protection of the nation."

An act of the Michigan Legislature of 1909 placed the former site of Fort Michilimackinac, on the southern mainland, in the hands of the Mackinac Island State Park Commission to become a tourist camp and a state park. Its magnificent trees, broad avenues, and amusement pavilions near the water's edge offer a strong contrast to the imagination in reflection on the terrors of the life of the place more than two hundred years ago.

The states of Ohio, Indiana, Illinois, Michigan,

Old baskets, bead and tendon work, of Chippewa Indians.

Showing construction of the dome shaped lodge. From Bushnell.

When Michigan Was Young

Wisconsin, and a part of Minnesota were carved out of the old Territory of Michilimackinac, upon whose soil Jean Nicolet was the first white man to set foot. The great enterprise of his life was the development of commerce. Nothing, even though it required the heroic courage of the most daring, daunted this man of almost unsurpassed bravery. For the enrichment of New France and for the furtherance of the commercial interests of the homeland, he staked his all, and for humanity he gave his life, for it was in an attempt to reach a persecuted Indian friend that he lost his own life in the waters of the St. Lawrence River, in 1642. What more had man to give? In memory of Nicolet the Michigan Historical Commission, the Mackinac Island State Park Commission, and the City of Mackinac Island have placed a bronze tablet near Arch Rock, on Mackinac Island. Although rich, and dignified as a reminder, yet the commonwealth of Michigan, heir to the region of the Straits, might well pause as it did in the year 1934, to do honor with ceremony and pageant to its first great leader of commerce, Jean Nicolet; and as a further and more permanent acknowledgment of his part in the founding of the great commercial life of the state, a monument befitting his courageous deed might well be placed on ancient Iroquois Pointe in his honor by the nation.

Chapter Twelve

The Last Guardian of the Straits of Michilimackinac

On the afternoon of the 9th of September, 1909, about a thousand people were gathered in Marquette Park, beneath ancient Fort Mackinac on Mackinac Island, at the entrance to the Straits of Mackinac in northern Michigan, to pay homage to a man who had given his life to bring the light of Christianity to the aborigines of North America. More than two hundred years ago Pere Jacques Marquette had come into the wilds of Michilimackinac to preach the gospel of Christ, and had spent a part of the winter of 1669-70 on Mackinac Island while superintending the building of a church at the Pointe, or village of Taenhotentaron, now St. Ignace, as it was the neutral meeting place for all Indian tribes of the Straits region.

The afternoon was one that could hardly be forgotten by those who were privileged to be there. The sun shone brilliantly over the green park and upon the white walls of the old fort above it on the hill overlooking the spot.

When Michigan Was Young

An air of solemnity and peace pervaded the place as people spoke in hushed voices as if in the actual presence of the remains of a beloved friend. There were no flowers, only the bright green grass, the gleaming white fort, and the waving Stars and Stripes above it, and only a few hundred feet away the blue waters of the Straits gently washing the shore where Pere Marquette must have landed from the birch bark canoe in which he first came to Mackinac. And today a beautiful bronze statue of the good Pere Marquette was to be unveiled in commemoration of the great accomplishments of his life.

The idea of erecting this memorial first came into the mind of Mr. C. B. Fenton, a Detroit merchant who spent his summers at the Island, as early as 1878, but it was not until the year 1899 that an organization was formed to develop the plan. At this time concerted plans were formed with both Islanders and summer residents officially organized to raise the funds and carry the project to fruition.

Now after more than thirty years the result of their efforts was about to be presented to the residents of Mackinac Island and the State of Michigan. Special invitations had been sent to President Taft and to several hundred other prominent men and women throughout the nation, and many of these people had come from far away parts of the country to be present on this notable occasion. There were dignitaries of the Catholic Church and of many other denominations, several of the country's most outstanding historians and leaders in other cultural professions, and there were people in lesser walks of life, all assembled in deep reverence as of one mind, to accept this tribute as a sacred gift to the people of the nation. The heavy cord holding the enveloping canvas covering the statue was pulled by Mrs. Maxwell Reynolds, grand-

The Last Guardian of the Straits of Michilimackinac

daughter of the late Hon. Peter White of Marquette, Michigan, who had been largely instrumental in financing the expense of the memorial. Miss Joplin is now Mrs. Maxwell, of Marquette, Michigan.

As the unveiled majestic bronze figure became revealed to the assemblage a feeling must have surged through more than one mind in that vast group that this was not only a symbol of recognition for the sacrifices of Pere Marquette, the great missionary, but for his mother country, France, that had sent so many thousands of her sons to open this western land that we might find freedom within its borders, and to the hundreds of young churchmen who gave their all in the sacrifice of self in this far away new land.

The Marquette statue measures twenty-five feet, including the pedestal. It was cast in Florence, Italy, after the design of Signor Trentanove. The weight of the bronze figure, which is ten feet high, is ten tons. It rests on a simple pedestal of Italian granite with a base of concrete. The cost of the statue was $5,950, at that time a very large sum of money. It was accepted for the State of Michigan by governor Fred M. Warner, who was introduced by the venerable Bishop Foley of Detroit, acting chairman of the day. Following Governor Warner, Justice of the Supreme Court of the United States William R. Day, acting as representative of President Taft, spoke with deep feeling and high praise for Pere Marquette and the noble band of zealous Christian men who came to New France with him to give their lives for love of their fellowmen. Justice Day's talk was a scholarly masterpiece of thought and high ideals.

Rev. Jonathan Cunningham of Marquette University in Wisconsin, folllowed Justice Day with a historical resume of the life of Jacques Marquette from the time when a boy of seventeen he began his life work in his homeland across the sea in France. Father Cunningham recalled the fact that the historian Bancroft had said "The people of the west shall raise up a monument to him," and it was with much pride in the telling that one of the foremost workers in the enterprise, Charles B. Fenton, told of the fact that the west had fulfilled the prophecy.

Tributes were also paid to the ceaseless efforts of Dr. John R. Bailey, historian of the Island, and B. F. Emory of the Mackinac Island National Park Commission in furthering the work of the Pere Marquette Statue Association.

In strange contrast to the residence of Pere Marquette on the Island nearly three hundred years ago surrounded by hundreds of uncivilized Indians, it was noted that less than fifty Indians were to be seen in the park for the unveiling. And they were thoroughly modern men and women no different in appearance from the rest of the assemblage.

Looking out over the water toward the great west that he thought to conquer spiritually, as Nicolet had conquered it commercially, the statue of Pere Jacques Marquette stands today on the shore of Mackinac Island. A beautiful park, once the old fort garden, surrounds the statue which is placed at the foot of the eminence crowned by Old Fort Mackinac. Under the flag of the New World the majestic figure of Pere Marquette stands, a lone guardian of the peace of the Straits of Old Michilimackinac, as if to forever bless this most beautiful spot in the ancient Inner Empire of Ottawa Land.

PART III

PEOPLES AND CUSTOMS
STORIES AND LEGENDS

Chapter Thirteen

The First Families of Michilimackinac

Who were the first families of ancient Michilimackinac, the Ottawa Inner Empire, and where did they come from? Known history finds the answer in the story of the Ottawa and Ojibway nations, although there are traces of an earlier race of people who lived about the Great Lakes. It is also known that these two nations separated from their parent nation, the Algonquins, who lived in the country north of the St. Lawrence River, several hundred years ago when they were engaged in a war with the Iroquois. They were driven from one location to another until finally they reached the region of the Great Lakes. The Ojibways settled on the lands about the Sault Ste. Marie, while the Ottawas moved on down to the Lake of the Illinese, or Lake Michigan.

The Ottawas had been known as At-a-wa-was while with the Algonquins, and after the English came into the country Henry Schoolcraft tells us that Ojibway was changed to Chippewa. When the break in the Algonquin

When Michigan Was Young

alliance occurred several other small nations also started toward the south and eventually joined the Pottawatomies living in the southern part of the Michilimackinac country. The Iroquois, leading the Five Nations from what we know as western New York, where their headquarters camp was located, had adroitly split the Algonquin tribes to weaken their defense, and succeeded in completely dividing that great confederacy for all time and driving the Algonquins back among their lakes and rivers north of the St. Lawrence.

We have learned earlier in this book (Part I—Michigans Historic Past) that the French fur traders first heard of the Ottawas as a nation that had gone "Out-aways," and called them "O-da-ways." The French Jesuit missionary Charlevoix called them "Ottawas," giving the broad sound to the vowel "a", and that has been the accepted name ever since.

Henry Schoolcraft, the Indian historian, affirms that Ojibway was the original name of another nation that became separated from the Algonquins, and that Chippewa was an English corruption of the name. Schoolcraft's information was first hand, through his wife Jane, who was a daughter of John Johnston, a fur trader who had married one of Chief Wa-bo-jeeg's daughters at Sault Ste. Marie. Mrs. Schoolcraft was educated at the mission schools and was a student of Ojibway history as well as a charming writer of both prose and literature translated from the Ojibway language. Schoolcraft generously gives much credit to his wife for his great fund of Indian history and legends.

Pressed by the Iroquois, whom all Indians feared, Wa-bo-jeeg migrated from the country about Sault Ste. Marie to the country bordering on the Straits of Mackinac, bringing a thousand warriors and their families with him. It is said that the passage of this great convoy down to the Straits took many months to accomplish.

It is difficult in the present day to imagine the transportation of several thousand people and tons of baggage many hundreds of miles by water in the frail birch-bark canoes used by the Indians. They were handy affairs because of their lightness, for they could be carried easily over the many portages that had to be used in traveling. Made of light bark, they were apt to be damaged if not skillfully handled. Necessity had made the Ottawas and Ojibways experts in handling any kind of water craft.

The batteau was a boat that became more used as the fur trade increased, for it was larger and had been improved by the French. Dug from the half of a large tree it was called a "dug-out" by the fur traders. Heavier and more cumbersome to handle, it was more used by the white men than the Indians who clung to their "sorrie canoes" as one early writer commented. The pirogue was obviously the heavy-duty boat as it was capable of carrying several tons of cargo and a dozen or more people. Though made from the trunk of a large tree, it had numerous improvements brought into use by the French, and also had a sail made of bark and animal skins. These boats were the only means of transportation on the Great Lakes and rivers for more than a hundred years, carrying millions of dollars worth of furs from the hunting grounds to the trading posts located about the lakes, and later as settlers and towns became numerous, doing the cargo carrying of all kinds of goods and products. In fact, until the middle of the nineteenth century it was not thought that this interior country would ever depend upon other than water transportation and the building of ships for the purpose became the biggest industry of the territory.

The Ojibways and the Ottawas long had been allies. It

is related that when they first met in battle both tribes were surprised at the similarity in their languages, and were so pleased that they threw down their weapons and became fast friends and allies. So the warriors of Wa-bo-jeeg were received by the Ottawas of the Straits islands and mainland as friends and allies. As the years went on intermarriages and joint hunting expeditions through the long winters brought them more closely together until today in Michigan one is never certain whether an Indian one meets is an Ottawa or an Ojibway.

It is the Indian's nature to be secretive, subtle and noncommittal. The early Indians would even change their names, or the name of their tribe, to fool the trader or missionary. They were superstitious and devoutly religious in turn, having a theology and mythology of their own. Every star in the heavens, every wind that blew, and in fact every action of nature conveyed a hidden meaning to them. It is by these tokens that Schoolcraft based his belief in their eastern origin.

Mr. Schoolcraft also based his theories upon their belief in transmigration of the soul to animals and birds as leading directly to the Arabian and Sanscript theologies. He traced the Ojibway god, Monedo, and the Ottawa god, Maneto, back to the Greek deo, citing also the similarity of the Mexican and Astec teo in the roots of all of these words.

Andrew Blackbird, an educated Ottawa Indian of L'Arbre Croche, who traced his ancestry to the Underground Indians and applied their legends, was convinced of a Hebraic origin of many of the Indian races. Mr. Blackbird laid his claims to the uniformity of many of the ancient customs of the Hebrews and those of the American Indians. John C. Wright, another educated Indian writer of L'Arbre Croche, found distinct Chinese

The First Families of Michilimackinac

features and mannerisms identical between the Indians and the Chinese.

All of these theories of men very close to the Indian mind in their lifetime, combined with the more recent beliefs of ethnologists and recent research by students, point definitely to the belief that at least some of the Indian tribes of North America did come originally from the Asiatic countries and that the Algonquins, the parent nation of the Ottawas and Ojibways, were among these eastern migrants.

We are telling the story of the Ottawas and Ojibways because they were the real first families of Michigan. Their portion of the territory, divided by the Algonquin seceding groups who called themselves "The Three Brothers," once covered the entire lower peninsula of Michigan and no one knows just how much more. As the government of the United States divided off one strip of land after another from the holdings of the numerous Indian nations, treaties were made and annual payment of many thousands of dollars were made to the various tribes. In this manner the once great Ottawa nation was crowded into the upper half of the lower peninsula of Michilimackinac territory. Their central camps came finally to be located in what was later called the Arbre Croche country which extended many miles around the peninsula dividing Little Traverse Bay from the Straits of Mackinac, as these localities are now called.

During this period the present Mackinac Island was set apart by the Ottawas as their sacred isle. About its peculiar rock formations and picturesque hills they wove a series of fantastic tales into their inherited mythology which modern visitors love to believe are the real history of the Island. The story of Mackinac's change from a fairy island to play its part in opening the Straits

When Michigan Was Young

of Mackinac to commerce is both thrilling and interesting, and has been told in numerous well written books. Since it has been from the first so apart from the basic history of the Ottawas, it must always be considered to have its own history, we believe, and so we will return to the Ottawas and Ojibways of the Arbre Croche country.

As we have seen in the story of Michigan's Historic Past, Jean Nicolet was the first white man to come into the Great Lakes country in 1634. The next distinctive visit to the region was the arrival of Pere Jacques Marquette during the winter of 1667-1670 at the neutral Pointe, now known as St. Ignace. Whether Marquette visited the Arbre Croche Indians or not is left to conjecture, It is most doubtful, as he was busily engaged in erecting a church at the Pointe and eager to get started on his trip west with Jolliet. That he did visit the Island of Mackinac is a fact we know, and it is probable that one or more of his immediate followers spent some time at the central village of the Ottawa people, L'Arbre Croche, or Wau-go-naw-ki-se, the English equivalent of which is "The Crooked Tree." While the entire locality has been called L'Arbre Croche, central or "Middle Village" was properly called Wau-go-naw-ki-se, or sometimes spelled Waugonokezee. That a chapel or church was built there or very near there seems without a doubt as so many well known Ottawa traditions point to that as a certainty. A few of the ancient cabins are still standing at Middle Village, with their stout logs dovetailed or notched together without nails, and their hardwood floors and rafters deeply worn with age.

This historic village is still the home of several old Ottawa families, and some sort of religious edifice has existed there all through the years since the visit of Marquette to the Straits country. Had Pere Marquette

The First Families of Michilimackinac

lived a few years longer he would have accomplished his desire to establish a college for the cultural training of young Indians at the Pointe, St. Ignace. His death in 1675 set the progress of the Ottawa nation back many years.

It was not until the coming of Father du Jaunay to minister to their spiritual needs that they were once again brought into close touch with the better ideals of the white people. It is believed that this zealous priest, du Jaunay, labored about thirty years among the Indians at Mackinaw City and along the southern shore of the peninsula bordered by Little Traverse Bay. From the time of his departure in 1765 there were no missions in the locality until 1824 when Father Badin came into the Arbre Croche country. Since that time the Catholic Church has maintained its contact with the Ottawa people, having at the present time, in addition to the church and school at Harbor Springs, several smaller churches in the surrounding territory, with a mission church at Middle Village and one at Cross Village.

The origin of the name L'Arbre Croche has given rise to numerous legends regarding its location and how the tree became bent at the top, as all agree that it was. That it did exist, at least in the middle of the seventeenth century, seems to be undeniable. The oldest legend is to the effect that Ne-now-bo-zhoo, the superman of the Ottawa nation, reached up and bent the top of the tree over so that the warriors coming along the shore in their canoes might be directed to the central village, or Wah-go-nok-a-zee, near the place where the tree is supposed to have been located.

Another story claims that a small chapel was built on the shore not far from Wah-go-nok-a-zee by one of the earliest Jesuit missionaries, and because of its nearness to the crooked tree the place was called An-ami-wa-tig-ong, meaning, "at the tree of prayer."

Certain it is that at a very early date the entire peninsula dividing the Straits from the bay on the south, now Little Traverse Bay, was designated as the Arbre Croche country, and so used in reports of the Jesuits stationed anywhere on the peninsula. This peninsula is about forty miles wide at a point at the head of Little Traverse Bay, known as Menonnaqua Beach, on the south and ending at Mackinaw City on the north, while it tapers to the west some thirty miles to a point at the present Cross Village.

The Ottawa tradition claims that the head village of the Ottawas extended from Tehin-gaw-beng, no Cross Village, down the shore of Little Traverse Bay through the central village of Wah-go-nok-a-zee, now known as Middle Village, to We-que-tos-ing, or the present Harbor Springs. It is known as the famous long village where every family occupied a front lot, and where the Indians came by the hundreds with their families from the long winter hunt in the south to spend their summers in planting and raising their corn and drying their fruits for winter use. Here they enjoyed their summer holidays and their annual festivals with singing and dancing, much as the present occupants of the land are doing at the present time. L'Arbre Croche was in fact the first popular summer resort in Michigan.

During the centuries when these changes were going on in the life of the Ottawas, their customs and habits brought down through the ages were also changing. Hunting parties often going west as far as the Rocky Mountains returned with captives from western tribes. One of these groups of captives, much larger than usual, was to wield a strong influence upon the Ottawas. These were people of high intellect and very rapidly became

Statue of Pere Marquette on Mackinac Island commemorating that great missionary's work and explorations in the Upper Peninsula over two hundred years ago.

The First Families of Michilimackinac

assimilated with their captor nation. In later years these people, many of them descended from the Underground Indians, became leaders and even chiefs and other officials. Andrew Blackbird and his sister, Margaret Blackbird Boyd, of Little Traverse as it was then, were considered in the middle of the nineteenth century outstanding members of the Ottawa Nation. Little Traverse is now called Harbor Springs.

All early writers declare the Ottawas as a people to have been remarkably receptive to the teachings of the missionaries and the other white people attempting to modernize their pagan habits. The great Chief Pontiac was an Ottawa, and though we could not uphold his attrocities during what is called the Pontiac raids of 1763, we can but respect his abilities as an organizer and military tactician. Had he lived in modern times, with modern transportation and communication at his command, it is believed that his plans for recapturing his part of America for the native Americans might have been successful.

For no reason that has ever been explained, the Ottawas of L'Arbre Croche claimed that they were not told just when the fatal blow was to be struck at Fort Pequotenonce, or Old Mackinac, and believing themselves slighted by this oversight, they extended a helping hand to four of the inhabitants of the fort who managed to escape. Alexander Henry was one of these men and his story of this dreadful massacre is most vividly told by him and repeated in numerous accounts of that battle, considered the only real authentic story of the affair.

As there have been traditions of Ottawas returning from the western hunting grounds with captive Indians called Mound Builders in the early years of their settlement of northern Michigan, many people believe that there may be ancient mounds in the Arbre Croche region that will at some time reveal much more than is at present known regarding the occupants of that locality in those early days.

All ancient Indian nations were composed of smaller groups or clans, each having its own chief, elected because of his superior ability, war chiefs, sub chiefs, and usually an orator, besides counsellors and medicine-men and women. It is owing to this long array of officials that tradition has often bestowed the title of chief upon one not altogether entitled to that honor.

Captive groups were permitted to live by themselves and to continue as many of their family customs as their new abode permitted. The separation into groups was obviously for protection from hostile tribes. Entire families often lived under the roof of one teepee, as many as fifty or sixty of them, all near relatives. These family teepees were long narrow affairs much like circus tents, made of bark and animal skins and having a great central pole and smoke outlet, with numerous lesser outlets and smaller poles. Each family group lived in its own corner or division. All were in harmony and peace because of the strict discipline of the chief and elected or appointed officials.

After the Ottawas were settled compactly about the Straits and the upper Great Lakes region, the French fur traders and the English mixed with them freely. In many instances these young adventurers entered into marriage contracts according to the Indian rites and became adopted into the Indian tribes. The young Indian girls were often very beauiful and when taken among the white people at the trading posts became adapted to the life of the white people. It is a matter of history that many Ottawa and Ojibway half-breed girls were sent to Montreal and a few even to Paris to complete their education after attending the mission schools maintained by the French in Michigan Territory.

About the middle of the nineteenth century a treaty was signed between the federal government and a delegation of Ottawa Indians, who were sent to Washington to protest against a decree that they were to be sent to a western reservation. As a result the federal government not only gave them back certain lands about Grand Traverse Bay and Little Traverse Bay, but also gave them the status of citizens of the United States with full voting privileges. This has proved to have been a very wise decision. There are several Indian schools still in operation in out-of-the-way localities, but most Indian children attend the regular grade and high schools of the state, some of them going on to college. They are usually diligent students, learning easily and having wonderful memories.

During the Civil War a full company of L'Arbre Croche Indians served with credit under the command of General Grant. Andrew Kag-a-be-tang, an Indian from the ancient village of L'Arbre Croche, was the first soldier from Emmet County in World War I to give his life for his country, while quite recently the remains of several Emmet County Indians have been returned from the battlefields of Europe and the South Pacific islands.

That the Ottawas and Ojibways are attracted to the industrial life of the state is evidenced by the fact that it has recently been reported that there are at least one thousand of them living in the city of Detroit. Many hundreds more are scattered about the state, but their roots are still implanted in the ancient L'Arbre Croche country in Emmet County, Michigan, where many of the descendants of the first families of the Ottawa and Ojibway nations continue to live much as they did before white people came among them.

Chapter Fourteen

What's in A Name?

A study of the early treaties between the white men and the Indian nations is a most fascinating experience. First, of course, is the reader's amazement at the abandon with which the Indian permitted his part of the agreement to be worked out by the white man entirely to his own advantage. As an old Indian once said, "white man he wanted to be allowed to sit on shore, then he wanted to take land little farther back, then some more, until now white man he got 'most all of Indian's hunting land." And so it was, as can be seen plainly even with casual reading and observance.

Then there came the question of signatures. The Indian had no written language. Tribal customs, rules of living, legends and theologies and mythologies were all passed on by wise men, orators and prophets. To the present day one may hear in the cabin of an aged Indian "my gran'fadder tole me" with the same affirmation that we say "once upon a time" when we tell our chidren stories.

They kept their traditions alive with marvelous faithfulness. Their many sign languages and signal codes will always be a mystery to white people.

When it became necessary for the white man to put into written words what he thought the Indian said to him, he was obliged to do it by translating phonetically, and hence the very strange sounds that he thought he heard sometimes turned out to be just the opposite in their true meaning. All this caused much confusion until the Jesuit priests began to take the matter seriously, and with their knowledge of the ancient languages of the east and much common sense they worked out a talking and a written medium of contact. But few ever went far enough into the real science of the native American languages to leave us readable books or dictionaries. Henry Schoolcraft did leave some interesting studies in grammar and comparisons with the ancient languages, and several other writers have helped with their conclusions, but we cannot get away from the fact that we have lost our chance to possess sufficient language translations to give us a really perfect basis for historical study of our aborigines. We hardly know as much of the true Ottawa and Ojibway foundation history as we do of the Mayans of Guatamala.

Among the interesting things found in the old treaties is the betrayal of the nationality and culture of the agent or secretary doing the writing. In one very old treaty the writer, evidently feeling that it was all just a form and didn't matter much anyway, drew funny sketches of the Indian's tribal animal, and had the Indian make his mark beneath it. Again he signed such names as "The Duke of York", "Daniel Webster", "Henry Clay", and finally running out of celebrities, he just wrote plain "Jim." French, English, Spanish, and German interpre-

What's in a Name?

tations are all found confounded with Indian syllables when the translator could find nothing in his vocabulary to substitute.

Wisconsin today would scarcely claim an acquaintance with its mixed French and Indian ancestor "Ouisconsin," for the "Ouis" became a "Wis" when an American Congress transformed the "Ouisconsin Hills" of the earliest maps into the State of Wisconsin. "Miss" meant large to the ancient Ottawas and Ojibways, and so we find the first spelling of Michilimackinac using the Miss as a prefix, while it is still retained in Mississippi.

It is said that one French missionary in the Michilimackinac Province baptized eleven hundred Indians at one time, and gave them all Christian names. Since he was a Frenchman, we find no Smiths, Browns, or Joneses among our northern Michigan Indians. But we do find an alibi for the missionary in the following names encountered by a missionary among the Ojibways of Michigan's upper peninsula in this twentieth century. The missionary calmly writes of his friend, an old chief called Ogemaheduhweekeezis and his companion Pahmekoomenahgakesheoongai; and again with the comment that these were oldfashioned Indians, he speaks of Ahkewanzemansquenner, and Mahnoonanuhwashkung. One would really dislike living among a thousand or more wild men and women bearing names of similar length and impossible pronunciation.

The reason for the great length of the Indian names is that they were always symbolical: Early Dawn, Long White Feather, Red Jacket, Flying Eagle, Big Cloud and dozens of similar names. Some of them when fully translated formed long sentences or even short paragraphs. In northern Michigan we have Pe-to-se-gay, or the Rising Sun, for the name of one of our fair cities; eventually it became Petoskey.

Perhaps no Indian name has suffered more from spelling and untrue pronunciation than the name of Michigan's beautiful Fairy Isle, Mackinac. According to Edwin O. Wood, in his "History of Mackinac Island," there are to be found sixty-nine spellings of the name in the Bureau of American Ethnology in the Smithsonian Museum in Washington, D.C. The name was borne as Missilimackinac, or Michilimackinac, for more than a hundred years by a considerable portion of what is now the United States. These sixty-nine spellings are listed as having been used by writers and publications of prominence all over the world during the three hundred years since the discovery of the Straits country by Jean Nicolet.

The French seldom pronounce the final consonant following a vowel. This makes it easy to understand how they came to leave off the "nong" that was first used at the end of the word, Missilimackinong, and substitute 'nac' in its place. "Nong", or "nac" pronounced in the French manner gives us a syllable that produces the sound "naw." The first English arriving in the Province of Missilimackinac interpreted the sound literally and gave the country the name of Michilimackinaw. Then, attempting to give it the French sound, they added a 'k' after the 'c' to finish it off, and that letter 'k' has tormented the word ever since in pronouncing the name, although it disappeared from the spelling along with many other "k's" used in colonial days by the English settlers in America.

This custom of using the final 'k' after a 'c' was brought to America by English-born Americns in the eighteenth century and it has not entirely disappeared even in our own day. The famous English writer, Samuel Johnson,

What's in a Name?

made much use of this final 'k' in his dictionary where one finds the words Atlantick, Potomack, frolick, and sarcastick and other similar words. As late as 1618 we find that H. M. Branckenridge, an American writer, in his history of "The Late War between the United States and Great Britain," frequently used the 'k' after 'c', evidently using the Johnson dictionary as a guide.

About fifty years ago, Andrew J. Blackbird, an educated Ottawa Indian who wrote a notable little book called "The History of the Ottawa and Chippewa Indians", declared that the name of the Island of Mackinac was first called "Mi-shi-ne-mack-i-nong" by the Ottawas in honor of the miraculous escape of two lovers of the "Mi-shi-ne-mack-i-now-go" tribe whose massacre and utter efacement by the Seneca's in their island home in Lake Michigan occurred many, many years before the coming of the white people into the country of the Lakes.

The legend claims that this young couple found refuge on Mackinac Island and lived there many years as guests of the Ottawas, whose allies their nation had been. Blackbird's explanation of the two names is that the name given to the Island is the locative case of the tribal name.

Mr. Blackbird's ending of this legend is also interesting. He tells us that the sweethearts were married according to the Ottawa rites and became founders of a numerous family living on the Island. They also became remarkably versed in the use of herbs for medicinal purposes, thereby incurring the jealousy of the regular medicine men and women of the Ottawas, and they determined to put the two old people to death. But, being under the protection of supernatural powers, they were warned of their danger and were assisted in accomplishing their disappearance from the Island by being turned into the "Wild-roaming-supernatural-beings," in the Ottawa language, "Paw-gwa-tcha-nish-naw-bay," or in our own language, fairies, thereby giving us the fairy type of legend that is always associated with Mackinac Island.

The first distinct change from the ancient Indian name is noted in the French Relations sent back to France by the Jesuit missionaries when the word was spelled Missilimackinac, construing the first syllable as meaning "great," something unusually large. That spelling was retained as the name of the entire Province of New France in America until the capture of Quebec by the English in 1759, when the first syllable was changed to "Mich."

It was left to Dr. John R. Bailey, resident historian of Mackinac Island, to tell us in his own way how to pronounce the name of the Island. After presenting numerous spellings of the name, Dr. Bailey says, "Now if you only get the 'nac' of it you will be able to 'naw' the word." That gives us our clue to the spelling and pronunciation adopted by the United States post office department. The ancient spelling and pronunciation was given the Island, and the city on the southern shore of the Straits was given the spelling "Mackinaw," thereby facilitating the postal service. And so Mackinaw they are both pronounced, or should be, though one is spelled Mackinac, retaining the old French spelling, as the Islanders themselves prefer it to be. Even more accurately historical will the pronunciation become it the "nac" is given a slight nasal sound, almost returning to the ancient 'nong' of the Indian nations.

Chapter Fifteen

The Passing of the Neuter Nation

The desire of a people living in what is now the United States to be neutral toward their neighbors is not altogether a modern idea. The early French voyageurs found such a nation of Indian hunters ranging the forests bordering the lower St. Lawrence and from the great falls to the "further lakes." It is supposed that they were a branch of the Onguiaahra, or Niagara nation, but from their indisposition to war on their neighbors the French traders called them the "Neuter Nation." Andrew Blackbird, the Ottawa Indian historian, relates the story of the Mush-co-desh nation, conquered and finally absorbed by the Ottawas of Arbre Croche, as having lived apart from other nations on an island in Lake Michigan for several hundred years. All these nations were originally a part of the great Algonquin Confederacy, but for one reason or another had separated themselves during the centuries from the parent group and formed smaller nations of their own. From the writer's research and studies the conclusion has been that the Neuter nation was a group from which the Mush-co-dish were separated.

The Jesuit priest, Daillon, wintered with the Neuter nation the winter of 1626-27, and the Relations of Brebeuf and of Chaumonot, 1640, refer to them as "A people larger, stronger and better formed than any other savages." They are described as having deep affection for their dead, and a love for their homes and families surpassing that of other Indians. For their entertainment they kept fools, or jugglers, in their villages and made merry with happy childish delight.

Forty villages were inhabited by them, and in these both Huron and Iroquois met on neutral ground. At the beginning of the seventeenth century they numbered twelve thousand souls, with four thousand warriors. These, however, preferred hunting to the warpath and by a common understanding formed commercial relations with the French that lasted as long as they remained a nation. They were zealous hunters and keen in the chase which often extended to the far west where so many rich fur bearing animals existed that were unknown to the Great Lakes region. The French traders paid for these priceless furs in blankets and stinted rations, and a generous supply of rum, and sold their booty at lavish prices in the courts of Europe.

An early writer eloquently compares these wonderful people to "A calm and peaceful island looking out upon a world of waves and tempests." To the east of them the fierce Confederacy of the Six Nations, with its western outposts of Senecas, controlled the right-of-way to the Hudson, and to the west the Huron Confedercy drove them back to the islands of the Great Lakes. That they became greatly scattered before their final defeat and

The Passing of the Neuter Nation

extinction is more than probable, for their characteristics can be traced among the Ottawas and Ojibways of the Great Lakes region, where hunting, fishing, and husbandry and peace have always been leading characteristics. But ask the warriors of the Huron and the Iroquois what became of the Neuter nation. If they were among the living today they could tell you a tale of stealth, of crafty warfare, of a deliberate plan for the extermination of the Neuter people. "Fight either against us or with us," their ultimatum ran, "but fight you must. What do we care that you have not schooled yourselves in the warcraft of your grandfathers as you should have done instead of hunting the wild things of the forest." And so after many generations of pastoral peace in their island homes and in ranging far-away forests in the freedom of the hunt, the Neuter nation was massacred by the deadly Huron and Iroquois warriors. Only a few hundred managed to escape in their canoes to the mainland where they eventually became absorbed by the Ottawas and Ojibways.

In less than half a century after their strength and mental superiority had been related as one of the wonders of the new world by Brebeuf and Chaumonot, they had become extinct as a nation. When La Salle came to the Great Lakes country in 1669 he failed to find this friendly nation of which the good fathers had written and he was deeply disappointed to learn that they had been effaced from the earth as a nation because of their lamentable unpreparedness in the face of hostility all about them. The passing of the Neuter nation is an age-old story of the sacrifice of the weak by the strong, of the perishing of those who preferred luxury and ease to preparedness and defense in time of danger.

Chapter Sixteen

Corn, the Indian's Staff of Life

Did corn or the Indian arrive in North America first, or did they come together? These are questions that have puzzled those who are always in search of the why and wherefore of everything they contact. Most people who believe that the Indians came from the Far East believe that they brought the corn with them. This thought is based upon the fact that corn forms a part in their most ancient rituals and religions. It guided their destinies, gave strength to their warriors, and was used in their early sacrifices. With the eyes of artists they adored the long silken tassels and the beautiful green husks. Even in the coldest of climates they planted and cultivated their corn with the utmost care, for it was their very staff of life. An interesting story is told by a missionary who lived among the Ojibways of the northern peninsula of Michigan more than fifty years ago, about an ancient garden of which an aged Indian told him. It was deep in the forest where the trees were several hundred years old that the old Indian had come upon a garden that he declared must have been made before the trees were seeded. There were signs of rows and hills under the leaves and brush and other evidences of what must have been a garden ages before his time. The old fellow declared that he had seen "with a skinned eye" the very pit in the ground where the corn had been stored.

Both the Ottawa and the Ojibway nations have a legend they told in their different ways of explaining how the Indians got the first kernels of corn, or Mon-da-min, for planting. One of these tales runs in this way: An Indian was wandering through the forest many, many years ago in search of game when he met a little man with a waving red feather in his topknot. As they approached each other the little man said to the Indian, "Take hold of me and remove my blanket," and when this was done he told the hunter to remove the red feather; then he bade him to remove all the little raised rough spots on his body. The little spots turned out to be kernels of Mon-da-min.

"Now if you'll break up my body you will find it will turn into pumpkin seeds." Then the hunter was directed to gather up all the seeds and to plant the kernels of Mon-da-min in hills in long rows on ground that had been neatly hoed, and the pumpkin seeds between the rows.

"When the planting is done leave the Mon-da-min to grow for the circle of the moon and it will be ready for the first hoeing. You'll be much pleased with its rapid growth and glad to hoe and care for it until it gives you long bodies like mine and each will be wearing a red or golden feather in its topknot."

While this advice was being given the little man with the feather had been invisible but his voice sounded distinctly among the rustling leaves of the trees.

The hunter did all the things he had been told to do and

Corn, the Indian's Staff of Life

found to his joy when the leaves began to turn in the squaw summer that he had a nice crop of ripe corn to provide his family and friends with food for the winter.

No other grain or article is as universal as corn among the Indians and aborigines of North and South America, being used so far as is known by all North American tribes and all along the western mountain chains and throughout the middle west.

The planting of the corn was a very ceremonious affair, so important that the braves themselves prepared the ground for the reception of the kernels that had been soaked in water until near to sprouting. All planting was done by women. The first hoeing, with a crude hand-hammered iron hoe, or wooden one if there was no iron available, was also done by the women. Careful cultivation continued throughout the growing time, varying according to the amount of moisture in the ground. When the time of full ripening came there was great rejoicing, particularly when the harvest was fine.

Then there was the drying of the big ears while still in the inner husks, the outer leaves having been stripped. The first colonists must have found the Indians drying their bunches of corn ears hung from the top of their teepees above the central fire, with the smoke, as the Indians thought, aiding in the curing as it passed out through the hole in the teepee used as a chimney. If the family planned to go farther south for the winter, great holes were made in the ground and lined with birch bark and leaves and many "mococks" of corn were dumped into it and stored for the family's return in the spring, to tide them over until the next ripening time.

The Indian women knew many ways of preparing corn for food. One of these ways has come down to us from our colonist ancestors as "hulled corn." The Indian method was to boil the corn in "peengwahboo" to soften the outside skin of the kernel so that it fell off. This "peengwahboo" was made of wood ashes and water just as our grandmothers made lye for the same purpose. After boiling in this water the corn was washed carefully and boiled again in pure clean water. And those who have eaten it in Indian homes say it is a very good dish indeed.

The Ottawas of northern Michigan had a queer-looking primitive mill for grinding their corn, which was always done by the women. The idea must have come down through many long ages, although to my certain knowledge these mills were used as late as 1875. The mill was a crude pestle and mortar. The mortar, or poodahgon, as they called it, was made from the trunk of a birch tree, perhaps a foot or more thick. This stump, or portion of the tree, was hollowed out about half way down its length, which was possibly five feet. The bark was left on to form a sort of binding, as barrel hoops are used, to keep it from bursting from the pounding of the pestle. This hollow was rubbed down smooth with a sharp stone. The pestle was a strange looking affair, with the center cut down to a thickness of about three inches and the ends left about twice as thick for a foot or more from the tip. The one I saw in front of an ancient Indian cabin, when I was a small child, had a pestle at least six feet long. It is possible that both ends were used for pounding because the rapid motion might cause friction and fire if used for too long a time. There seems to be no other explanation for this double-ended pestle.

The corn was put in this mortar, or poodahgon, and the Indian woman would grasp the pestle in the center with both hands and pound and grind the corn until it was all broken up, if intended for parching and eating as we eat cereals, or if for soup, only until the outer skin came off.

Corn, the Indian's Staff of Life

But if intended for what the southern Negroes call hoe-cake, the corn would simply be pounded until a fine meal was achieved. There is little doubt that the Negroes got their idea of hoe-cake originally from the aborigines of the south.

In the story of Mary Jemison, the white woman captive who lived with the Senecas over seventy years, she tells of pounding corn all night to prepare "samp" for breakfast for white officers who had come to their camp to hold a council. This samp was a fine sort of corn meal which was used for a porridge as we use oatmeal. We can well imagine that they also used maple sugar with it when eating it from the wooden dishes from which it was served. They used no tables, but sat on the ground wherever they were comfortable. Whittled sticks were used for spoons.

Because of their centuries of contact with the missionaries and traders, the Ottawas and Ojibways were more restrained and conservative than the western tribes. Their festivities, though often marred by strong drink, were seldom offensive during the eighteenth century. There were no snake dances or cruel sacrifices; all was under the strict supervision of the divisional chiefs, for each nation was divided into tribes, and the tribes into lesser groups.

Their corn dance was the great national festival, its gaiety and abandon depending upon the results of the harvest, for upon this their very lives depended. Bark ropes would be suspended from between trees and great bunches of ears hung on them to achieve decorative effects, while tall stalks of corn stood beside the teepee's entrance.

As much corn as possible was left over from the previous year to be used in making the favorite dishes for the big feast when every form of meat and fish obtainable was served "buffetstyle" on hand carved wooden dishes.

The Ojibways made a gala affair of the fall husking, and it may be from them that we derive our ancient husking bees in which the red ear played such a prominent part, for they too centered their frolic at the husking around the red ear. If a maiden found a red ear while pulling away the long outer husks, and it turned out to be a beautiful straight ear, the omen was that a handsome young brave was waiting nearby for the girl to throw it at him. But if the ear was found to be sharply pointed at the end, or if it was a crooked ear, the omen denoted the fact that a thief had been in the cornfield, and the laughter was loud and long, while the entire group shouted "wa-ge-min, wa-ge-min," a thief, a thief, and there was no lover designated for the girl.

Whatever the Indians did there were always songs to accompany the act. A favorite song usually followed the finding of the red ear.

Henry Schoolcraft's translation of the Ojibway red ear song is as follows; the chorus being sung first:
Chorus: Wagemin! Wagemin!

> Thief in the blade,
> Blight of the cornfield,
> Paimosaid.

Recitative:
> See you not traces, while pulling the leaf,
> Plainly depicting the taker and thief?
> See you not signs by the ring and the spot,
> How the man crouched as he crept in the lot!
> Is it not plain by the mark on the stalk,
> That he was heavily bent in his walk?
> Old man be nimble, the old should be good,

Corn, the Indian's Staff of Life

> But thou art a cowardly thief of the wood.
> Wagemin! Wagemin!
> Thief in the blade,
> Blight of the cornfield,
> Paimosaid.

The explanation of the last word is that it implied a man walking, one who walks in the night. Hence he came for no good and must have come to steal the corn. Several verses of like import followed while the gay husking group made merry as they paused in their husking to sing and dance.

As this was the one time of the year when all of the youth of the tribe were assembled in one place it seemed a good time for a serious gesture to creep into the fun, and one of the most revered and wisest of the older chieftains appeared among them to give them a lesson in wise living and the better ideals of the tribe. This was done in the best oratorical manner of the wise man and was received with all due respect by the group. It was all part and parcel of the annual celebration and the festivities were quickly resumed as soon as the lecture was over, but were usually a trifle more subdued as befits such an occasion.

The use of the name Cornplanter must have been a favorite one, like our Charlie or John, for we find it in almost every Indian nation of the eastern and middle western confederacies.

The artistic value of corn in decoration was fully realized long before white settlements were formed in Michigan, according to an early missionary among the Ojibways. He had managed to get a tiny church erected and on opening day, which he had selected at our Thanksgiving time, and explained why very fully to his congregation, he entered the church after an absence of several days to find the entire interior bedecked with long corn stalks, bunches of corn leaves and clusters of silken tassels mixed with sprays of wild red berries from the forest. "It was truly beautiful," he declared.

Even to the present day an Ottawa or Ojibway garden has its space carefully kept for corn whether other things have room enough or not, and a visit to their cabins in the fall will always disclose the big bunches of ears suspended for drying from the rafters as nearly as possible as it used to be in the forest teepees of their ancestors. For now, as in the ages past, corn is their staff of life.

In recent years the Indians have made very pretty and substantial mats of the dried corn husks which they often color with the gay dyes with which they dye their woven baskets, bright reds and greens being their favorite shades. Usually the husks are braided and then sewed firmly into round mats, sometimes several feet in size. Also the husks are saved and used for kindling and numerous other purposes such as scouring cooking dishes.

An ancient custom, too, that seems to be as popular today among the white folks while picnicking as it was among the Indian, is roasting the big ears of corn in hot ashes before husking. Just dip a green ear in water for a few minutes and then cover it snugly with the hot ashes of your bonfire and you'll have a delicious picnic morsel, though it does smear your face and hands with black wood ashes. The ancient Indians had no cows, and so no butter. If they required more than the softening of the steam from the husks we may imagine that they made use of the rich fat of wild animals that had been stored away for such an occasion, for our native Americans were very thrifty people.

An evidence of their frugality was the manner in

Corn, the Indian's Staff of Life

which they planned for the long trip each winter on their hunting expeditions when the entire family went along if able to do so. The very old and feeble and the sick remained in the summer camp where everything possible was arranged for their comfort through the long winter. For the hunters and their families canoes were loaded with many mococks filled with corn meal, ground corn for cakes, and corn in every form used by the group. Also there would be big mococks of maple sugar and dried berries.

If the trip was to be made by land, a carrying sled, or travois, would be loaded with these provisions. The travois, a name given the conveyance by the French, was made of two long slender poles bent while green to form both runners and shafts. Split poles formed the floor of the travois, crossing from runner to runner, and being held firmly with straplike thongs made of animal hide. This hide was also used to form the harness attached to both shafts and pony. For Indians always had ponies, procuring them from the hundreds of wild herds they encountered on the western plains during their winter hunting trips.

An old squaw usually did the driving, often with a papoose in its cradle on her back and several other children happy on the fur robes among the mococks. Their teepee poles were rolled in their birch bark covering and stretched along the travois; they could set up their lodges in a few minutes, and proceed with the making of their preparation for a meal for their braves with little effort. Indian women considered these things as a part of their housekeeping or homemaking, just as hunting and the warpath belonged to the man. While no wife was permitted to walk before her husband, the prohibition was regarded as his right because it was his business to lead the way, and his business must not be usurped.

Chapter Seventeen

The Legend of Ne-Naw-Bo-Zhoo

The Ottawa Indians have a legend, believed in implicity by the earlier generations, ragarding a very strange being whom they called Ne-naw-bo-zhoo, a personality embodying characteristics resembling the central figures of many different narratives of the Old Testament. At times we find him regarded almost as a god, at others as a very mischievous individual, causing people all sorts of troubles. Again, a person of unlimited powers, a veritable Paul Bunyan of the ancients. As a matter of fact he might well be the prototype of that fabulous character of the lumbering days of Michigan, his deeds were so prodigious and fantastic.

We are much indebted to Andrew Blackbird, the Ottawa Indian historian, for the most descriptive story that has been written about this mystical being. Using Mr. Blackbird's somewhat tangled tale of Ne-naw-bo-zhoo's doings as a basis, an attempt will be made to record some of the remarkable performances of this

When Michigan Was Young

legendary hero.

The legend starts off in the spirit of a religious tale, bringing the infant Ne-naw-bo-zhoo into the world as Christ came, the child of a virgin mother. At the same time a twin brother was born to this mother, who came into the world with all the embodiments of a monster-child of evil, whose coming took the life of the mother, who had been ragarded as a sort of sainted person.

As the mother of Ne-naw-bo-zhoo had lived in the home of her grandmother the child was now mothered and raised by her. But the monster-child fled from the tee-pee as soon as it was born and was never seen again by living man, although his evil deeds were often encountered. As the child Ne-naw-bo-zhoo grew to boyhood his actions were so unusual that the grandmother said to him "Your actions are like a Ne-naw-bo-zhoo." And the boy replied "I am the great Ne-naw-bo-zhoo upon the earth." The meaning of this word to the Ottawas was a "clown," a sort of god of tricks. And of course that introduces one of the many contradictions of character into the legend because the Ottawas construed his meaning as being that he was the great clown of the world.

As he grew to manhood he became a great prophet, and at the same time a skillful hunter, always followed by his favorite dog, a massive black wolf. It was at this time that he learned of the story of his brother, the monster who had roamed off out in the world to do evil things. He determined to follow and kill him if he caught him. So he sharpened his arrow flints and saw to it that his great warclub was in perfect fighting condition, and then he set forth on his quest about the world. As he went he tested the war club and found that one stroke from his mighty arm felled the largest trees. Whenever he came to a huge rock he would test the might of the club and

The Legend of the Ne-Naw-Bo-Zhoo

hundreds of chips of flint would fall to the ground, so that always afterward wherever chips of flint rock were found the people of the forest would say, "Ne-naw-bo-zhoo has been here."

Now the story of the flood is introduced. It seems that the god of the deep was very jealous of Ne-naw-bo-zhoo's having such a fine hunting dog as the black wolf. So he lured the dog away from its master and killed it and there was a great feast given by the killer who invited the sea-serpents, sea-tigers, and all the other monsters of the sea to the feast. Ne-naw-bo-zhoo determined to kill this dreadful sea-monster. The water gods were in the habit of sunning themselves on the shore at a certain sandy spot, and it was here that Ne-naw-bo-zhoo decided the deed must be done. Accordingly he disguised himself as a stump after seeing to it that his strong bow and arrows were in readiness, and waited for the arrival of the sea-monsters. The wiley sea god was suspicious and sent several scouts out to investigate the shores, fearing a trap may have been set for him by Ne-naw-bo-zhoo. But the stump made no sign, not even when one of the serpents twined itself around its base and nearly squeezed the breath out of it. So they went back and reported that the stump was harmless and they all came ashore and settled down for a nap on the sand. Now was Ne-naw-bo-zhoo's chance, and he set his best arrow into his bow and shot the sea-monster right in the heart.

A terrible commotion followed and all the other sea-monsters like a host came up on land and began to chase Ne-naw-bo-zhoo. For once the great clown was frightened and realized that he must call into his service some miraculous thing to defeat such formidable enemies. He ran, and ran, and ran all over the face of the earth, while waves of water like mountains pursued him, always

When Michigan Was Young

growing larger and larger. So when there was no more dry land for him to run to, he commanded a big canoe to be built by the spirits of the super-natural world. And it was built and Ne-naw-bo-zhoo and all the animals that had fled from the sea-monster with him got into the canoe and it floated safely on the top of the waves.

As they rode at the will of the waters Ne-naw-bo-zhoo began to wonder how deep the water was, and where all the land had gone to. So he sent a beaver down to see, telling him to return with earth in his paw. But the poor little beaver died before he could reach the bottom. When he came floating to the top dead, apparently, Ne-naw-bo-zhoo blew into his nostrils and he came back to life, so we still have the beaver. The muskrat was next asked to go down for the earth, but he didn't want to go after seeing what happened to the beaver. However, he was flattered by being told that he was the best diver of all the animals and he decided to go for the earth. He too had expired before he returned to the surface, but in his small paw he clutched a bit of earth, to the great joy of Ne-naw-bo-zhoo, who revived him.

And now the strangest thing happened, for this great half-god, half-clown of the Ottawas had taken a raven into the canoe with him, and now he made the bit of earth brought up by the muskrat into a tiny parcel and fastened it around the neck of the raven and told it to fly all over the face of the waters, and they would begin to recede. So the raven flew back and forth all over the waters, and, sure enough, the earth did begin to come back just as it was before, and all the animals, birds, and people went about their business as if nothing had happened.

Ne-naw-bo-zhoo also figures as a hero in a tale whose analogy could have been no other than the ancient tale of Jonah and the monster-fish. The Ottawa legend runs

The Legend of the Ne-Naw-Bo-Zhoo

that a great serpent lived in a lake where the Indians liked to fish. He was a very cruel, vicious serpent who chased the boats that went out on the lake, and sometimes swallowed them, Indians and all. Of course, this terrified the people who had to go on the lake to fish, for they depended upon the fish for their daily food. To help his people, the Ottawas, Ne-naw-bo-zhoo decided again to do something about it. "This great fish will eat up all my nephews," as he called the Indians, said Ne-naw-bo-zhoo, and so he sharpened his weapons and went out in his boat and began to sing taunting songs to the serpent fish, Mish-la-we-gwe. Presently the fish came along and swallowed the boat and Ne-naw-bo-zhoo along with it, and that was just what the daring clown wanted, for he began at once to torment the stomach of the serpent and continued to prick him with his weapons until the serpent was almost driven crazy and, trying to get away from its agony, it ran right up on the beach and expired on dry land. Whereupon Ne-naw-bo-zhoo walked out of his mouth and went home and sat down calmly to smoke his pipe, feeling that he had saved many people from a terrible death brought about by the sea-serpent or monster-fish.

There are numerous other tales told regarding this clown-god, all of them similar in basic ideas to the narratives of the Old Testament and its ancient tribal rulings. Whether these tales were brought to America from the east or were woven into legends from comparative tales told to the Indians several hundred years ago is problematical. Whatever the truth may be, it is an uncontested fact that the earliest white men found many similarities between the natives of America and the Eastern peoples, not only in customs and legends, but in manner and features, while often encountering identical words in Indian and the languages of the Orient.

Chapter Eighteen

Pokagon's Village

Many years ago there was a secluded Indian village on the shores of a beautiful clear blue inland lake in the depths of a great forest in northern Michilimackinac. It was a beautiful spot, and its residents were what was called in the vernacular of the white settlers and back-woodsmen, "Honest Injuns." Why they had chosen this hidden retreat apart from the big settlements of the Indian nations was never known, probably because they were a group of simple peace-loving people and wished to pursue their arts and to live in their own manner.

One legend declares that they were a remnant of the Mushcodish tribe that escaped from the Ottawas when that tribe was supposedly completely effaced by the Ottawas several hundred years ago. The story tells us that a small group of families managed to creep away into the forest and to find their way many miles back to this Clear Lake where they settled permanently. But the Jesuit priests knew where they were and ministered to their spiritual needs, and so the little colony prospered. Probably about three hundred acres comprised their settlement, and this tract of land came under one of the early treaties after the United States took over Michilimackinac Province. As has been stated in an earlier story, the Indian agents were very careless regarding these treaties. Too often the names written beside the Indian's mark, which was a picture crudely drawn of his tribal totem, was not easily legible. A moose might look like a deer, or a dog like a rabbit, and the white man cared little about what this was going to do to the Indian's descendants a century or two later. It is doubtful if these Indians ever had even a scrap of paper describing their dealings with their Great White Father. This little story is being told to record the unhappy events that were the result of this lack of efficiency in an early day in Ottawa Land.

About sixty years ago it was possible to rent a small steam launch for a day, and with a private party of a dozen or more friends cruise this lovely Clear Lake during a long delightful day, and many summer tourists took advantage of this pleasure. A string of rowboats trailed along behind the launch, and several times during the day there would be a stop at a small dock beside the lake for a drink of cool spring water from some gurgling stream, and several of the sightseers would do a bit of fishing by the way. It was one of the very great days of the tourist summer vacation, this idyllic trip on the inland lake. And not the least of the joys was the stop that was always made at Pokagon's Village. Pokagon had been gone many years by this time, but

Pokagon's Village

he was living at the grand old age of a century and more when the first settlers came into the country.

But the spirit of Pokagon and his kind remained in the village. The people of Pokagon's Village were industrious and skillful, and many of them very artistic in their handicraft. The ancient cabins had been built before nails were commonly used, and were notched and dovetailed together with a splendid idea of exact fittings. Fine pieces of hardwood were used for the casings about the openings.

The missionaries had taught their Indian friends how to do these things in the manner of the white man, always adapting the plans to the Indian patterns. The little backwoods cabins were actually works of architectural art, and so they had stood through sun and stormy weather as firm and perfect as when built centuries before. And Pokagon's people followed the pattern of their cabins. Each family had several acres about its cabin where corn and pumpkins and other foods and a bit of hay for their ponies were grown. Beside each cabin in summer was a neat pile of basswood for the basket-making that the women of Pokagon's Village did more beautifully than any other workers anywhere about. Their porcupine quill work was also the finest in the inland country.

Long before the white men came to strip the great forests of their beauty there was a Catholic church in the center of Pokagon's Village, and no doubt whether a priest came to visit them or not, the Indians held their own religious services in their own way as their missionaries had taught them to do.

When the launch appeared on the lake its occupants could see the Indian women running from their cabins with big bundles of baskets, rush rugs and mococks, and

Ottawa Indians making miniature elm bark canoes to be sold in a nearby village. Their cabin was built entirely without the use of nails.

exquisite birchbark boxes ornamented with clever designs of colored porcupine quills. They all gathered in one of the larger cabins to await the arrival of their guests. Then the people from the launch would troop up to the cabin and the bartering would begin. It was great sport. No doubt much more would be paid in the end for the pretty treasures than would have been for the same thing down in the big white village. But everyone was happy and had a wonderful time, while the owner of the launch assisted by some of the men gathered up enough wood to carry the launch on its way.

It is recalled that an amusing incident took place on one of these occasions. In the cabin where the trading took place one of the men spied an ancient looking tomahawk hanging on the wall. The man was intrigued; he must have that instrument of murder. He decided not to leave the place until he had secured it for his own. His first approach to the Indian interpreter received a decided repulse. "Ka-win Ka-win, (No, No), Dad mine Gran'fadder's, me not sell heem," and the parleying went on, until at last after an outrageous price had been determined upon the buyer became the winner, much to the disgust of one of the women, who did not hesitate to express her dislike for the entire transaction. "Why did you let him have it?" she asked the Indian as she lingered behind the rest of the party to express her sympathy. Coyly came the reply from the oppressed Indian, "Ump, me, I mek me anudder," just as the clever rascal had probably made that one. The "Honest Injun" had learned at least one of the arts of the white man's manner of trading.

Would you like to see this Arcadian village beside the lovely Clear Lake in the big green forest? Well, that joy is one of the things that northern Michigan has sacrificed

Pokagon's Village

to the greed of man. The village is gone from the face of the earth, ruthlessly torn and burned to the ground when the Indians refused to leave their beloved homes. They had lived in unconscious freedom in the belief that taxes were the white man's concern, that they were in no wise interested in them, for had not the Great White Father said in the treaty that they were exempt for all time from taxation? They believed it, and had lived generation after generation unmolested, just as many other groups of Indians lived all over the state of Michigan, because there had never been a man with a mind so small that he could bring himself to disturb them.

At last a man did come along who coveted the land and particularly the great virgin forest surrounding Pokagon's Village. His lawyers craftily looked up the back tax lists and he was easily able to find a perfectly legal loophole that had been overlooked for so many, many years because so many men had really had a sense of the fitness of things and an aversion to defy the laws of God and nature. And the man, of course, won the land, and mercilessly drove the inhabitants off from it. The years have gone on and the ancient village land has passed from one owner to another and so many changes have been made in its pattern that all that is left is a little cemetery half grown over with weeds. The descendants of the old families resting in the cemetery, many of them with a reluctance born of real sentiment, have in some way secured tiny plots of land back from their beloved Clear Lake and continue to live their simple industrious lives. To their great honor several of their young men have served in both of the great World Wars, and one has recently been returned from overseas to find his last resting place with his forefathers in the old cemetery of Pokagon's Village.

Chapter Nineteen

The A.B.C.'s of the Reverend Peter Doughtery

With the entrance of Michigan Territory into the federal group of the United States as the State of Michigan, settlers began to move into the frontier regions of the state. The knowledge that Henry Schoolcraft, executive Indian agent of the territory, had been doing a good job amalgamating friendships between the Indians and white settlers had much to do with their confidence in the future of the new state. It was with the conviction that his efforts would be supported by Schoolcraft, that the young graduate of Princeton, the Rev. Peter Dougherty, came into the Grand Traverse region to start his missionary career in the year 1839.

Mr. Dougherty located at a point now known as Old Mission and established a school and church for the Indians of the region. Schoolcraft at once sent a farmer to the mission, which was under the direction of the Presbyterian Foreign Missionary Society of Philadelphia, and this added advantage appealed strongly to the

When Michigan Was Young

Indians who joined whole-heartedly into the scheme to forward modern civilization.

No attempt will be made in this little story to tell of the struggles and trials of the young missionary, but we will record the fact that his efforts were well rewarded with the splendid success of his work, and the lasting impression that it left on the people, both Indian and white settlers, with whom he spent many years of devoted service. During these years the Rev. Dougherty established other missions in the north country, one of them being the mission of Muh-quh Se-bing, on Bear Creek in Emmet County.

Beside his duties as religious instructor and school teacher the young preacher was often called upon to act as legal advisor, and even as doctor to people and beasts. But along with these ordinary duties he never lost sight of the fact that he had received more than an ordinary education for the foundation of his work, and in the quiet of his own cabin in the great wilderness he gave many long hours to deep study of the language and dialects of his Indian friends. In particular was he interested in the Ojibway language. As a result of this study in orthography two tiny volumes written by the Rev. Peter Dougherty were in use in the Muh-quh Se-bing, or Bear Creek Mission in 1852. Extracts and comments from the little hymnal, and from "Easy Lessons in Scripture History" by the Rev. P.Dougherty, will form the basis for the continuation of this story.

Perhaps the most interesting fact in the books is the conclusion of the compiler that the Ojibway language uses but nineteen letters of the accepted modern alphabet, eliminating the sounds of seven letters, **c f l q r v x**. Both Ottawas and Ojibways being descended from the Algonquin nation, we may assume that this would explain

The A.B.C.'s of the Reverend Peter Dougherty

to a very great extent the extremely puzzling differences in early translations of the Indian languages by the first invaders, the French, whose alphabet contains no **w**. And this particular letter was a favorite of the Ottawas and Ojibways in the formation of their lingual sounds, though of course they were unaware of its values, as they had no written language other than their signs used on totems and trees, and occasionally on pieces of birch bark peeled and cut to a neat thinness.

The Rev. Dougherty proceeds to give, in a preface to the Ojibway Hymns, or Ojibway Nugumoshang, of which there are forty-two old and well beloved hymns of the Protestant churches, the vowel and diphthong sounds as he translates them. It is a most valuable bit of work that seems to have been lost sight of in the history of the aborigines of Michigan. The hymns are all written in both English and Ojibway, using the sounds as he translated them with the elimination of the seven letters that we consider so essential to our English language. That this backwoods student missionary was so successful in expressing the English thought and language so perfectly in the Ojibway language without these sounds, seems a most remarkable achievement. Several of the hymns are given as illustrations of Mr. Dougherty's splendid work in orthography. The Hymnal was published by The American Tract Society about 1845, and the "Easy Lessons on Scriptural History" by Rev. P. Dougherty in 1847, by John Westfall and Co. for the Presbyterian Board of Foreign Missions.

Except for ten short lines under the word "Key" the writer starts right in with his lessons covering the well known Bible stories from Adam to the Day of Judgment with numerous added features and lessons in religious living, altogether using some seventy pages in a small book for the entire Catechism. In all of these lessons the student preacher adheres to his rule of using his nineteen-letter alphabet, and comes out gloriously victorious in his efforts. The translations are most amazing, and the meanings very simple and clear, a feat that it is doubtful if a less well informed and profoundly enlightened student could have accomplished.

As examples of the translations of Rev. Dougherty the first two pages and the last two are given in both English and Ojibway, as found in the "Easy Lessons."

FIRST LESSON

Adam

Who was the first man?
Adam.
Who made him?
God made him of the dust of the earth.
Where was he placed when first created?
In the garden of Eden.
Did he stay there long?
He did not.
Why did he not stay there long?
Because he disobeyed God.
How did he disobey God?
By eating of the forbidden fruit. Gen. II:16, 17.
What did he do after he had eaten the fruit?
He tried to hide himself.
Was not this very foolish?
It was: "for the eyes of the Lord are in every place, beholding the evil and the good." Prov. XV:3.
What became of him and his wife after they had sinned?
They were driven out of the garden, and obliged to work

The A.B.C.'s of the Reverened Peter Dougherty

very hard.
Did God tell Adam that he should die?
He said, "Dust thou art, and unto dust shalt thou return."
What name did Adam give to his wife?
He called her Eve.
How long did Adam live?
"And all the days that Adam lived, were nine hundred and thirty years; and he died." Gen. V:5.

OJIBWAY

Ah-Dam

Wa-nan dush ow kah-ne-tuh-me-ah-ne-ne-wid?
Ah-dum suh.
Wa-nan kah-o-zhe-od?
Ke-zha-mun-e-do suh o-ge-o-zhe-on we-yuh-guh-sa-e-wuh-ne-nig eu ah-ke.
Ah-neu-de dush ke-ah-sind ah-pe wah-yash-kud wa-zhe-ind?
Ke-te-gon-ans-ing suh E-den a-zhe-wen-dag.
Kin-wazh nuh e mah ke-duh-ne-ze?
Kah-wen.
Wa-go-na dush kin-wazh ka-on-je duh-ne-ze-sig e-mah?
O-ge-guh-gon-ze-tuh-won suh Ka-zha-mun-e-don.
Ah-nen dush kah-do-dung ah-ge-guh-gon-ze-tuh-wod Ke zha-mun-e-don?
O-ge-me-jin suh eu kah-go-tuh-mo-nind a-de-tag.
Ah-nen dush kah-do-dung kah-e-squah-me-jid eu a-de-tag?
Ke-ge-je-a-e-we we-gah-zod.
Kah nuh wen ke-guh-ge-bah-de-ze-se?
Ka-gat; e-nu mah wen osh-kenzh e-gon ow Ta-ba-nin-gad min-ze ah-yah-ne-wun wah-bun-dung eu muh-je-

ah-yah-e-wish gi-ya eu wa-ne-zhe-shing. Prov XV:3.
Ah-nen kay-e-zhe-wa-be-zid ow e-ne-ne gi-ya e-nu we-wun kay-ish-quah muh-je-do-duh-mo-wod?
Ke-zah-ge-je-nah-zhah-kah-wah-wug suh e-mah ke-te-gon-ans-ing nun-dug-wah dush ke-ge-zhe-ah-no-ke-wod.
Ke-zha-mun-e-do nuh o-ge-wen-duh-mo-won e-nu A-dam eu-ka-gat zhe-ne-bood?
Ke-e-ke-do we-yuh-guh-sa-ing suh ke-ke-on-de-ne-go, me-nah-wah dush go na-yob ah-king ke-guh-e-zhe-ge-wa.
Ah-nen dush kah-e-zhe-ne-kah-nod ow A-dam e-nu we-wun?
E-ve suh o-ge-e-zhe-ne-kah-non.
Ah-nen dush me-nik kah-be-mah-de-zid ow A-dam?
Mah-mah-we dush e-nu o-ge-zhe-go-mum ow A-dam shong-uh-swok ah-she ne-se-me-ten-ah tuh-so pe-poon ke-be-mah-de-ze: me dush ke-no-bood. Gen. V:5.

THE LORD'S PRAYER

Our Father, who art in Heaven, hallowed be thy Name; Thy kingdom come; Thy will be done on earth as it is in Heaven; Give us this day our daily bread; and forgive us our trespasses, as we forgive those who trespass against us; and lead us not into temptation; but deliver us from evil, for Thine is the Kingdom, and the Power, and the Glory, for ever and ever. Amen.

THE LORD'S PRAYER

No-sa-non ish-pe-ming a-yah-yun gwa-tah-me-quan-dah-gwuk ke-de-zhe-ne-kah-zo-win; Ke-do-ge-mah-we-

The A.B.C.'s of the Reverened Peter Dougherty

win tuh-pe-ah-yah-muh-gud a-zhe-min-wan-duh-mun; mah-no tuh-e-zhe-wa-bud o-mah ah-keng, ish-pe-ming gi-ya; me-zhe-she-nom suh non-goom ke-zhe-guk kuh-ba ge-zhik kah-o-buh-qua-zhe-guh-ne-me-yong, gi-ya wa-be-nah-mah we-she-non eu nim-bah-tah-e-zhe-wa-be-ze-we-ne-nah-nin, e-zhe-wa-be-nah-mah-wung-e-dwah e-gu ma-je-do-duh-we yuh-man-ge-jig; ka-go guh-gwa-de-ba-ne-me-she-kong-in ning-uh-je zhe-sho-be-ze-yong; gi-ya me-tah-gwa-ne-mah-we-she-nom muh-je ah-ye-we-shun; ken suh ke-te-ban-don eu o-ge-mah-we-win, gi-ya eu kush-ke-a-we-ze-win, gi-ya eu be-she-gan-dah-go-ze-win, kah-ge-nig gi-ya kah-ge-nig. Ah-men.

Rev. Dougherty had an assistant in compiling the "Easy Lessons," a Mr. D. Rodd, and between them we find several **q's** tucked into the script. But we forgive them this license as no man is infallible, and neither could dream that a close scrutiny would be made of their work a hundred years hence. It must have been most difficult to entirely eliminate the 'q' as it occurs so often in the modern Ojibway language. And then there is always that ancient alibi, a typographical error. Even at that the translations are nothing less than marvels.

HYMN

1

From all that dwell below the skies,
Let the Creator's praise arise;
Let the Redeemer's name be sung
Through every land, by every tongue.

2

Eternal are thy mercies, lord,
Eternal truth attends thy word;
Thy praise shall sound from shore to shore
Till suns shall rise and set no more.

3

Praise God, from whom all blessings flow;
Praise him, all creatures here below;
Praise him above, ye heavenly host;
Praise Father, Son, and Holy Ghost.

NUGUMOWIN

1

Ku-ken-ua-king a-a-jig
Tu-ma-mo-yu-wu-gan-dum-og,
She-nu-nu-gum-o-tou-a-wat
Ga-ge-zhe-kum-ag-o-wa-jin.

2

Ka-ge-nik tab-wa-mu-gut-on
E-neu ke-dik-e-to-win-un,
Tu-mud-wa-non-da-goz-e-wug
Miz-e ga-ma-mo-yu-wa-jig.

3

Ma-mo-yu-wum-a-ta, ma-bum
Wan-je-sha-wan-da-goz-e-yung,
Wa-os-e-mint, wa-gwis-e-mint,
Gia Pa-niz-it O-je-shag.

The A.B.C.'s of the Reverend Peter Dougherty

It is the belief of the writer that the contribution of the Rev. Peter Dougherty to modern civilization cannot be estimated alone by his work either as a minister of the Gospel or a teacher in his backwoods school at Old Mission, but as the discoverer of a most valuable connecting link between the aborigines of the great Inner Empire of Michilimackinac and modern civilization in his translations of the A.B.C.'s of the Ojibway nation.

A case in point may be the Ottawa and Ojibway sounds to represent the word Michilimackinac, as that word was first pronounced by the French invaders of the Straits region. "Miss" to the aborigines meant great, and that syllable still provides the first sound of the name applied to the great waters of the Mississippi. The French, entirely familiar with the sound as "Mich," at once applied to the ancient Indian name. From that day on confusion and confounding of sounds gave all voyageurs, priests, travelers and laymen trouble in tagging localities and tribes with their true names. To the present day this maze has never been untangled. It would not be surprising in the least if some zealous linguist in the future years, by means of the Dougherty A.B.C. system, develops a key to the hidden secrets of a little known period in the ancient history of the peoples who inhabited the great Inner Empire of Ottawa Land in which are located many of the most populous and important states of the Union.

All of the middle western states retain as place names of many of their most important cities and towns the ancient Ottawa and Ojibway names, if not in the original form, in spelling closely related to the aboriginal concept. The meanings of these names and their historical values might well be worked out to a clearer understanding of them with the aid of the Dougherty system of aboriginal spelling.

Chapter Twenty

Muh-quh Se-bing

or

The Bear Walk

Many, many years before white men came to live in the great forests of northern Michigan the beautiful blue lake several miles southwest of La Petit Traverse was called Muh-quh Se-bing by the Indians who hunted for game in the forests. These Indians were Ottawas and Ojibways, friendly tribes who had lived together in peace for more than a hundred years. They also gave the winding, twisting creek carrying the overflow water from the lake to La Petit Traverse the same name because to them it was where "the bear walks," literally where there were plenty of bear to be had for the hunting beside the running water.

Muhquh Sebing was only a small part of a larger country called at times Tonadagona, and at other times

When Michigan Was Young

Kashkauko, by the white men many miles away who settled such matters and made the maps. White men have a strange habit of just walking into another man's country and changing things around to suit themselves.

Well that's the way it must have been about the name they gave to this northern forest. The old chief, Kashkauko, never lived in the Muquh Sebing country, though some of his relatives did. But they were good Indians, while Kashkauko was a very bad man whom the white judges had decided would have to be hung, but the legend is that he took his own life instead. However, it was not long before Kashkauko too was changed for another name.

This time another man who lived on an island in Lake Michigan called the Big Beaver, where he attempted to form a permanent Mormon colony, decided that he wanted to call the forest Emmet, because he was an Irishman and was fond of the poet Robert Emmet. As he had gotten himself elected to the Michigan legislature he persuaded the people at Lansing, the State capital, to call the forest Emmet County, including most of what are now known by several other county names bordering on the present Emmet County. This man was the first real politician in Emmet County. His name was James J. Strang, but he called himself King Strang, and he really wanted to found a kingdom instead of a colony. The project was defeated by his assassination by a follower whom he had flogged for disobedience.

While all of this was taking place, covering a period of some years, a number of Ottawa and Ojibway families from the north side of the bay, now known as Little Traverse Bay, came to live on the south side at Muhquh Sebing. They were mostly Indians of the Protestant faith and were great lovers of freedom of thought.

Muh-quh, or *The Bear Walk*

There is something about the lakes and forests and the great expanses of free land in America that makes a man want to be an "American" just to set foot upon the soil of it. How truly free these native Americans must have felt because they and their ancestors had once owned all the land about them.

They had learned of a missionary who had a school down on Grand Traverse Bay where Indian women and girls were taught to cook, and sew, and keep house like the white women; and boys and men were taught to till the soil and make things grow, and to make many things that white men used about their homes and farms. So they piled their pots and pans and blankets into their canoes and set sail for Grand Traverse Bay to find out what it was all about.

But they didn't like it in that country. It was too crowded, and they missed the great forest where Muhquh Sebing gave them good hunting. And they decided to make one more appeal to Washington for their old lands. With this end in view two of their wise men, Chief Mwake-we-nah, called Daniel Wells by white men, and Andrew Blackbird, an educated Ottawa from Arbre Croche, were selected to go to Washington to intercede for them. The Indians must have been very persuasive for they got what they wanted, and that was a return to the Indians of a large tract of land in the Muhquh Sebing and Arbre Croche localities.

There had been a number of treaties between Washington and the Indians of Northern Michigan but this was the most liberal one of all. Each head of a family was to be granted eighty acres of land in Emmet County if he would occupy the land, and each of his sons was to be given forty acres. This, to men who had now found a way to till and make use of the land, seemed like a very good idea; and many of the wise and thrifty Indians took up the offer of the white father in Washington and selected their lands around Muhquh Sebing.

But who was to teach their children how to clear and plow, and plant and reap? That was a serious matter. So away they went, back to the good man on Grand Traverse Bay and begged for a teacher to live among them and to do all of these things. Andrew Porter was the young missionary teacher selected by the Rev. Peter Dougherty from his staff at the Presbyterian Mission School on Grand Traverse Bay, to undertake the task of establishing a school and teaching the Indian boys and girls at Muhquh Sebing.

Andrew Porter and his family came into the Muhquh Sebing country in the spring of 1852 just when the snow was leaving the land and the pussy willows were pushing gently out from the branches. It must have been a strange experience for these Pennsylvania young folk to travel from Chicago by boat to Mackinac Island and from there by sailboat to Muhquh Sebing, where there were nothing but Indian cabins nestled among the stumps on the half cleared farms. At first they had to live in the home of Daniel Wells until a home could be built for them on a hill a half mile from the bay. And of course the small schoolhouse must also be built. It was officially known as Bear Creek Mission School.

It must have been during this time that the Porters heard of the meaning of the name Muhquh Sebing, the bear walk, and they probably were told of the belief that some of the Indians still had, that certain members of the Indian tribes could turn themselves into animals in the forest at will. For there are Indians in the Arbre Croche country on the north side of Little Traverse Bay who even in our day, believe it can be done.

Muh-quh, or The Bear Walk

The story was told by a young Ottawa woman not so long ago, that her grandmother could actually become a bear if she wished to. As this story is in keeping with the belief of the Indians in transmigration no doubt a similar story was told the young missionaries who were to live in the Muhquh Sebing country.

The history of the Porter Mission School for the next twenty years is a story in itself. This is the story of Muhquh Sebing from the time when a group of Ottawa and Ojibway Indians came to live in the forest where the bear walked beside the creek until authorities in Washington once again got their eye on the forest and made up their mind that this was just the place for the veterans of the Civil War. This time the Indian settlers were paid for their land.

The Grand Rapids & Indiana Railroad had recently laid its rails into Traverse City and there were rumors in the air that the main line running north from Grand Rapids to Walton would soon be moving toward the Straits of Mackinac. And so there was much big talk.

A year or so before this railroad idea began to spread through the north country several changes had taken place in Muhquh Sebing. First, a white man, Hazen Ingals, had come with his family to live beside the creek not far from the mission school. Then the Presbyterian Board of Missions in Philadelphia had decided to close the mission, and another white man, Nathan Jarman, came to live in the Porter home with his family and to till the mission fields. Hazen Ingals had eight sons and two daughters and seemed to have quite a bit of money, for he at once bought several of the old Indian farms and orchards.

The white men had ideas of their own about these lands and promptly platted a good many of the acres into lots and once again changed the name of Muhquh Sebing to Emmet City, hoping no doubt that the terminal of the prospective railroad would be located in this village, already platted and laid out in streets. There was a Cahtolic church that had been established about the time of the Porter Mission, several white families, a grist mill, a saw mill, a grocery store, where Hazen Ingals sold pins and soap, and buttons and thread, and groceries to the Indians, and a saloon kept by John Ingals, the oldest son of Hazen.

They were not reckoning with a fur trader, Hiram O. Rose, who owned nearly a mile of lime ledge up the shore of the bay east of Muhquh Sebing. Mr. Rose had been one of the contractors in connection with building the railroad into Traverse City, and knew very well the men who were now contemplating pushing the road on north toward the Straits. Also, Mr. Rose owned a trading post across the bay at Little Traverse, now Harbor Springs, and formerly when the Indians lived there before the white people came, We-que-to-sing. This post, or store, where clothing and blankets and food were traded to the Indians for furs, was managed by a Mr. Burbeck, Mr. Rose's father-in-law, and it was with her grandparents that Abbie, the twelve-year-old daughter of Hiram Rose, was to stay that August of 1873 while her father and several officials of the Grand Rapids & Indiana Railroad held a pow wow with a group of the leading Indians of Muhquh Sebing.

They had all come by sailboat from Traverse City and the men were prepared to remain until the pow wow could be brought to a satisfactory end. Abbie, however, declined to go with the boat to Little Traverse, insisting that the Indians might scalp her father if she left him. Finally, arrangements were made for the little white girl to be

Muh-quh, or The Bear Walk

cared for in the home of Ignace Pe-to-se-gay until the pow wow was over, which everyone thought would be within a few days. An Indian pony was provided for her pleasure and she roamed about the Muh-quh Se-bing country in perfect safety, spending much time at the little school conducted by the Porter Presbyterian Mission on a farm about a half mile back from Little Traverse Bay. She was to come later with her parents to be one of the first white settlers in the new village which was platted in 1874.

Although, Captain Rose, as the officials called Mr. Rose, spoke the Ottawa language fluently the pow wow lasted six weeks. At its close much of the land owned by Ignace Pe-to-se-gay and his sons had been sold to Captain Rose or the Grand Rapids & Indiana Railroad officials, and the Pe-to-se-gays had agreed to plat the rest of their lands into lots in the new village of Petoskey, so named for Ignace Pe-to-se-gay, now called by all of the negotiating parties Chief Petoskey.

When the new village became a reality those who had platted their lands under the name of Emmet City, a village that had never been incorporated, joined the corporation on the east side of Bear Creek and gave up the name of Emmet City.

To the Indians the mission school was the Muh-quh Se-bing Mission, but to the white people it was known as the Bear Creek Mission. Now with the village of Emmet City, in which the mission was located, coming into the village of Petoskey, the date of the real start of the new village traces back to the establishment of the mission in 1852, some twenty-two years prior to the final platting of the modern resort city of Petoskey in 1874.

The little mission schoolhouse and the Porter home are still standing on the Jarman farm, reminding us of the early efforts of the white man to bring civilization to the Indians of Northern Michigan.

And the beautiful little city of Petoskey on the shores of Little Traverse Bay now stretches far to the east and west and south of what was once the forest of Muh-quh Se-bing, and fertile farms surround the ancient site of the Indian village and the beautiful lake now called Walloon, with its river flowing toward the bay now known as Bear River.

Chapter Twenty-One

Joe Francis, Hero

The cabin of Joe Francis, seen from the shore drive two hundred feet above it, looked like a big black-and-white agate dropped down in the center of a garden. A nearer view revealed its ancient hewn timbers to be weather-beaten with age, and its ribbons of plaster chinking carefully and neatly whitewashed.

Surrounding the garden was a cleared plateau of about twenty acres that stretched to the shores of Little Traverse Bay. A long arm of sand, scarcely visible until you reached the shore, curved out into the bay to form a cove. Ugly rocks, scattered the length of this sand arm, gave warning of danger to a boat attempting to land in the cove in stormy weather, contrasting oddly with the quiet and peace of the garden where we caught an occasional glimpse of Joe and his wife at work among their vegetables, as we drove down the rutty hillside road one bright spring morning.

It is a quaint old place, with its flower and vegetable

garden outside, its half-orderly litter of small tools, a sleeping dog on a grassy plat in the sunshine, and its tubs and pails tipped up against the side of the house in neat arrangement. As Joe ushered us into the home-like furnished living room he stooped to cover a brood of tiny yellow chicks in a box beside the stove in the center of the room. On the other side of the stove a contented family of maltese kittens were asleep in another box.

Joe, well accustomed to such visits, knew that it was the story of the rescue that we had come to hear, and commandingly he said to his wife, with a courtly wave of his hand toward the loft, "Go get."

Mrs. Francis instantly ascended the crude, ladder-like stairs along the side of the room and presently returned with a rag-wrapped package that revealed, when untied and unwound, an embossed leather case, which she placed in Joe's hands.

Joe must have been a very handsome Indian in his day, and even though his face was now wrinkled with age it still showed remarkably strong character and dignity. And on the wall the crayon portrait of an Indian girl, well-dressed and good looking, to which Mrs. Francis pointed pridefully, told us that she too had come from more than an ordinary family. It was hard to realize, however, as she sat quietly by the table with her grey head bent over her bark and quill work, that she had once been young and pretty.

As he held the little leather case tenderly in his hands, Joe sat straight in his chair while he told us his story, at one moment assuming the dignity of his Ottawa ancestry, and again in the excitement of the telling embellishing the tale with a dramatic genius undoubtedly inherited from a strain of French blood flowing in his veins.

"Tirty year, dat's it, tirty yer next Sunday morning. I

Joe Francis, Hero

get up, see beeg storm on bay. Waves, he roll high lac hill. White on top lac snow. Come shore Little Traverse Bay beat rocks lac mad. Me, I long time sail on Lac Supe-ri-or, mek beg wave dar, no wave so high lac dees wave. Me, I see heem queek." And Joe leaned forward in a listening attitude, with his hand cupped at his ear. "Stop, me, Joe, I hear men's calling. Run 'long shore, listen, see boat on rocks. She's tippin' too, half down side in water an' tree men's deys tryin' hang on top side. Day see me 'long shore. Put han's to mouth, 'Halloo! Halloo!' day call."

"I call loud, 'I'm goin' get help,' Run woman, get help queek, sabe men's. Woman, she scare, no run queek. Me, Joe, I run to Indian man's house down Middle Village, 'bout half mile. Knock, knock, one, two, tree time. 'Joe, he say, when I shout and pound on door. 'What you want?' "

"I say, You John Williams, come queek with me. Tree mens, day drown. We got go on boat, sabe mens."

"John Williams, he say, 'what for, Joe Francis, I got to die mek white men's live. I no go. I sleep some more.' "

"I say, John Williams, I gotta sabe dose men's. You go on sleep some more."

"Den I go one, two, tree, meybe some more house. No Indian man, he can' see why. I mos' tired out. Den I find one man, beeg, strong, cut lots o' wood. He go. I say, meybe we die, you Jo Kijigobinessi, me, Joe Francis. You tink dat bes' we go?"

" 'Yes, we go,' he say."

"So we run queek to my beach. See mens still hold fast to dat boat's top side. No call. Pretty weak I guess. We got to hurry. Ain't got much time. Joe he run queek for big rope in my shed, while I get oars and push boat into water. Den Joe, he take one pair oars, an' me, Joe Francis, take odder pair and we work hard tryin' to reach dat boat out dar on dose rocks. Not much good, jes steer, keep boat straight goin' after dose mens. I tell you dose waves dey pret near toss my boat on sand-bar. We hear mens call, 'Help! Help!' Not loud dis time. Seems lac we ain' neber goin' get dar in time. Mens boat, shes beeg launch, jes jump right up and down an' pound against dose rocks. Guess didn't have 'nuf gas. Once Joe Kijigobinessi say, "Better we go back, Joe Francis, dat boat shes gone now.' Me, I say, 'Tawa nebber go back. You better ask big Chief up dar he help you an' me sabe dose mens.' "

"Clouds so black ober Lac Michigan can hardly see. Nor'west wind she blowin' lac hurricane. Mek dose waters pile up one wave on top nudder wave so fas' sometime my boat she seem lac leetle chip. Mus' be eight, meybe ten feet high, dose waves."

"Bime-bye beeg wave he lif' my boat up lac hands we not see, set heem down 'long side men's boat two, tree, meybe ten time. We try hard keep boat near, but sometime get 'way off from dose mens. Den me, I say, 'God, you wan' mens sabe? You do you mek boat still queek, I se one man he mos' gone now, we got hurry we sabe heem.'"

"Beeg wave, he stop roll 'bout one minute. Joe Kijigobinessi, me Joe Francis, we work fas' pull mens in my boat, all tree, 'for wave he go mad again some more. Mens day froze mighty near steef. Lie down in bottom of boat, no help. We got pull hard in such mad water. Me, I tell you I been sailor long time on Lac Su-pe-ri-or. Dat Lac he mos' rough water in world. I walk so, on beeg boat," and Joe threw back his shoulders to illustrate a great effort to keep straight up on his feet, as he continued, "Mek no fall down, always on feet. But dese waters more mad dan Lac Su-pe-ri-or."

"Jo Kijigobinessi, he lose oar gettin' mens in boat, so I

Joe Francis, Hero

say, 'You, Joe, tie mens fast so they no' roll out, tip us all obber, den you tek pail an' get all the water you can out of boat. Not much good, keep Joe warm meybe. So me, Joe Francis, I pull dose oars lac I nebber pull oars before, tryin' to mek dat shore fore we all go on rocks. My boat she good strong Mackinac, made good wood. I mek her myself, all one winter. Sometime she stan' right up so, lac tree; den she roll almos' obber lac log. Dose time I tink we ain' nebber goin' lan' on beach."

"Bime-bye one beeg wave he tro boat high on shore. Beeg rocks dey smash hole in bottom of boat. Ye bet me an' Jo Kijigobinessi we some glad lan' on dat shore. Indian mens, some women too, day mek han's togedder lac bed, carry mens to my cabin. My woman, she smart, she hab water hot, coffee too. Jo Kijigobinessi, me, Joe Francis, we drink 'bout quart 'fore stop. My woman, she no gib mens beeg drink. She smart medicine woman. She gib dees time jes leetle. She mek mens bed on floor ner fire. She watch 'em all night dat time. One feller, he no' move long time. My woman, she rub him and mek blood move, den sometime long in night he stir jes leetle, den she mek him drink hot coffee some more. Bime-bye he breathin' lac odder fellers, den she tell him sleep some more."

And Joe, relaxed now that the big rescue had been accomplished, stopped for breath. His great struggle to defeat the storm and to save the lives of the three men at its mercy, had been so vividly and dramatically portrayed and we had all been so keenly thrilled that the plaintive meowing of the kittens and the cheeping of the chicks had not been noticed. Now, as Joe's voice, still resonant and finely modulated, ceased for a moment, these sounds filled the little cabin like a chorus sung to the accompaniment of the gentle lapping of the waves on the shores of the cove, waters so quiet and serene today that they looked in their blue stillness as if angry elements could never have the power to disturb them.

Presently someone asked, "And what happened next, Joe?" For we were all anxious to see the inside of that small black case, still held tightly in Joe's hands.

"Why, mens dey stay by my house mebbee tree, four day. Berry weak, not walk much. Bime-bye feel better, go 'way. Lebe me, Joe, leetle money. No much pay. We guess ain' got much. Boat all smash up. I don' care. I don' mek sabe dat way." And Joe drew himself up proudly, "I mek sabe lac Heem up dar," as he pointed solemnly upward, "I mek sabe 'cause i got lub here," and Joe laid his two hands across his heart.

"Den," modestly came from Joe, "beeg talk in papers. Detroit, Chicago, den noting more mebbe tree mont'. Bime-bye come man, he ask, 'What you do Jo?' "

"I say, jes go boat, bring mens in."

"No," he say, "You mos' brave man on Leetle Traverse Bay, meybe state of Michigan too."

"I mek laugh, say dat funny joke he mek."

"He say, 'What you are Joe, Jibway, Tawa?' "

"I say 'Tawa, my woman, she Jibway.' "

"He say, 'Joe Francis, dat you name, all o' heem'?"

"I say 'Kawin.' "and Joe laughed as he sprang hi own Ottawa word for 'no' on us. "I say, 'My name, all o'heem, Joe Francis O-ke-no-te-go, nobody say O-ke-no-te-go, jes Joe Francis.' "

"Des man, he wan' know ebrything. Go out on shore. Look at my boat. Look at my lan' good and plenty. Tink house fine, need roof pret' bad. How much I owe? How much mek sell feesh, cut wood? How much eat? My woman she ain' got good dress. How much basket she sell? Den he say beeg Fadder in Washington, he got know pret' queek, soon."

"I no' care, I say all he wan', den he go 'way."

"Bime-bye come nudder man wid beeg letter. He say, 'Joe, beeg white man you sabe, he hab lots money, he pay taxes, feex roof, ebrything. Next mont' you get money. You no'work, you lib here in des ole place lac you' Fadder, you' Gran'fadder, res' you life. You good Indian. White Fadder and beeg man, dey fix it up.'"

Joe paused, then with simple dignity he went on, "Den, bime-bye, come to me, Joe Francis O-ke-no-te-go, dis leetle box." Joe touched the case in his hand tenderly. Then, as it opened at his touch, he handed it to the member of our party nearest to him, and as it went around the circle that we had formed about Joe we saw the man before us with a new feeling of awe and admiration, for none of us had ever before held in our own hands a real Carnegie Medal for great bravery. But there it was, a small bonze plaque inscribed with Joe's full name, the date, and the action that brought him this great honor. Was it any wonder that in his pride Joe had learned to tell his story with so much dramatic fervor?

"Did Joe Kijigobinessi receive a medal too?" our small boy asked.

"Yes, Joe Kijigobinessi, he hab a medal too. He good Indian man down Middle Village," Joe replied.

As we said good-bye to Joe and his wife and left the cabin we thanked him sincerely, and each member of the party left a token of appreciation in his hand.

"Bazh-wa-pek, Op-ta-wa-pek, non-wa-pek," we heard him reciting to his wife as he counted the coins, and then as if well satisfied with the day's work, "Me, Joe, I tell heem good, dat time!"